ENDORSEM

On five continents, in many countries, I have stood with Bill Johnson and worshipped our triune God, preached the Gospel, seen God heal the sick and deliver the demonized—all in our mutual pursuit of revival. I know of no one living who is more passionate about revival. Bill Johnson, as he says, "has no plan B," only plan A—revival. He is a man who has read about the great historical revivals, studied the leaders of such revivals, and laid down his own life to continue the heritage of revival for our day and generation. For the last twenty-five years he has walked in the fire of revival. He also is a primary cheerleader of the next generation of revival leaders. There is much to gain from *Open Heavens: Position Yourself to Encounter the God of Revival.* Buy it and read it. Feed your hunger for revival and build your faith for God to use you in revival.

Blessings in and through Him,

—**Randy Clark**
DD, DMin, ThD, MDiv, BS Religious Studies
Overseer of the apostolic network of Global Awakening
President of Global Awakening Theological Seminary

Bill Johnson has been a dear friend of mine for many years, and yet I am continually amazed at the grace of God on his life. Many people have written about revival—but Bill lives it. As a seasoned apostle, teacher, and author, Bill truly carries the spirit of revival in everything he undertakes.

His newest book, *Open Heavens,* comes at a timely intersection in history. Revival is on God's agenda, and the stage is now being set for a move of God unlike anything the world has ever seen. With invaluable insights into Scripture and personal God stories, Bill Johnson offers a unique glimpse into the heart of God, who passionately desires for revival even more than we do. If you want to experience more—and encounter the God of revival—you won't want to put this book down. The fires of revival are already burning, just waiting for you to run with them!

—**Dr. Ché Ahn**
President, Harvest International Ministry
Senior Pastor, Harvest Rock Church, Pasadena, CA
International Chancellor, Wagner University
Founder, Ché Ahn Media

I believe that we are not waiting for God, but God is waiting for us! Bill Johnson has walked the walk and is now called by God to make you normal. That's NORMAL according to the Bible.

—**Sid Roth**
Host of *It's Supernatural!*

If you are like me, when someone mentions the word revival many thoughts race through my mind. Years ago, I began my journey studying revivals in the past, the present, and what we can learn from them for the future. What I've learned over the years is that many Christians say they want revival but very few realize what that really means. And that was precisely the reason we began Revival Radio TV.

When I saw Bill Johnson was writing on this topic, I was intrigued by the title *Open Heavens—Position Yourself to Encounter the God of Revival* and I was eager to experience the revelation Bill received from the Father. I was not disappointed. There is so much here to glean. I pray you highlight the lines that God quickens to your spirit and review them often. This is indeed a book you will keep close by in your library!

One specific insight jumped off the page to me. Without a doubt, it is not the only revelation that you will glean from this rich title. It's a nugget hidden deep within the pages about small beginnings. While most believers (me included) are looking for the next Pensacola Outpouring, Azusa Street, or Welsh Revival, it is the small kindling that lights what is to become the roaring fire of revival, not the giant oak timbers. Revival starts small and when we as believers stop long enough to see it, we will see God pouring Himself out to those who are willing and desire Him more than ever, no matter what that looks like.

Most will not argue these are the last of the last days. Seeking Him is not only important for spiritual guidance, but it is essential if we're going to shine our light brightly in these times. Living under an open Heaven and encountering the God of revival is the best way to not only see the Father, but to let Him use you in a mighty way, right now. Enjoy the journey in this book as Bill Johnson lights the path.

—**Gene Bailey**
Revival Radio *Flashpoint,* host

Bill Johnson is a dear friend of mine. He is a man of deep humility and hunger for God. His love and kindness have marked my life personally. His love for Beni, his children, his entire family, his church and friends are a wonderful example to me. Bill's insatiable desire for more of God's presence is contagious. We've spent hours talking about Jesus together and His marvelous works. There are few voices on earth more suited to speak about revival. May Jesus' Kingdom flood the nations.

—**Michael Koulianos**
Jesus Image

Over the years we have seen what the Lord has accomplished in Bethel's passionate pastor with a great heart, truth-seeking mind, and intense passion for Christ and our lost culture. Going to speak there for one single session with such a massive collection of Heaven-hungry young people in one of their classes is like attending an explosively fiery, fun-filled football game jammed with God lovers and Jesus seekers drawn together in a common call to see truth touch our time again and righteousness return as reality. *Open Heavens* is not just a nice collection of significant truths about revival. It is also the stunning true stories and recurring risky records of one man's adventures with our astonishing Lord. This is the true essence of what revival is: His never-ending call for the courage to join Him in that ultimate mission in which He dares us to die to ourselves to help in each Millennia to save the world.

—Dr. Winkie Pratney
Author of *The Revival Study Bible* and *Revivals: Principles and Personalities*

Open Heavens is a presence book. I say that because one cannot read it without feeling touched by the presence of God. It will open your eyes to being able to walk and live in revival and transform your life and the culture around you.

—Cindy Jacobs
Generals International

Bill Johnson has authored many important books giving us revelation concerning our relationship with the God of revival. But this book will move you to a deeper understanding of "revival, reformation, and renaissance." Revival is not an end in itself but it opens up the greater dimensions of Holy Spirit and the effect it has upon not only the Ekklesia, but upon our culture and society. This book is a must read for those who are hungering for revival and more of Holy Spirit. Get ready for a greater conviction and revelation as you process this excellent book.

—Norman Benz, D.Min.
Lead Pastor, Covenant Centre International
Palm Beach Gardens, Florida

In over two decades of friendship with Bill Johnson, one thing that impresses me is his continual hunger to learn more about the Kingdom of Heaven. Though we each see and know in part, to seek the Lord daily for more wisdom is not optional for us—because we too live to call those around us to the life of Heaven, even and especially from some of the darkest places on earth. May this book inspire you to the same longing, the same great adventure, and the same joy in humble service.

—Heidi G. Baker, PhD
Co-founder and Executive Chairman of the Board, Iris Global

To live under an open Heaven has a twofold benefit: we'll live with unhindered access to God, and God will have unhindered access to earth. My friend, Bill Johnson, reveals how through bold faith and a life of unswerving obedience, we'll always bridge the gap between Heaven and earth.

—John Bevere
Bestselling author and minister
Co-founder of Messenger International and MessengerX.com

My heart leapt with excitement at the opportunity to read through the manuscript of Bill Johnson's latest book *Open Heavens*. I found myself devouring the book as each chapter fueled a deep hunger in my heart. It is my experience that this book carries an impartation for personal revival that is so special and so needed. Through his long experience of researching, living in, and stewarding revival, Pastor Bill brings us distilled wisdom and valuable teaching that we can all use to practically engage with and respond to the Holy Spirit's stirrings of revival. Bill's teaching on recognizing "the oak tree in the acorn" and "honoring the point" were just two of the many rich revelations that I found profoundly helpful and impacting. This book is a gift to leaders and believers who are pressing in to see sustained revival. Pastor Bill's beautiful descriptions of encountering God in revival atmospheres resonate so authentically with my heart. I believe that as you read this book, the heartstrings of your spirit will also begin to resonate with authentic worship and a hunger to know our wonderful God in deeper and more intimate ways. The Holy Spirit is calling us to get ready for the greatest revival the world has ever seen, and this timely book is powerful fuel for the fire.

—**Katherine Ruonala**
Senior Leader
Glory City Church

Revival will not come as a "flash in the pan," a short-term, "here today, gone tomorrow" momentary ego boost for the Church. Instead, God is moving us into lifestyles of burning and a sustained hosting of His presence.

Bill eloquently unpacks the concept that "there is no such thing as a week of revival meetings." Rather, it's a contagious, ablaze, ongoing journey.

This book will help you burn again for God and move you into active yielding and bending to the Holy Spirit, reawakening a longing for Jesus—at any cost. Bill's personal stories are honest and inspiring. As you journey with him, you will wrestle and be challenged by the need to put yourself into places of persistent prayer and movement to steward where God is going. After all, as you will read, "wise men still travel."

—**Emma Stark**
Director of Global Prophetic Alliance—Glasgow, Scotland
Author of *The Prophetic Warrior*

What a gift this book is. A handbook for the era and beyond. A treasure trove of wisdom and revelation that is priceless. A road map of wisdom to steward precious moves of His Spirit. This book has been penned by the Holy Spirit through Bill for such a time as this. This book is weighty;

it's a gem to be treasured, and a tool for the days we are in, where we will see revival and His Glory poured out and revealed in unprecedented ways. Thank you, Bill, for such an incredible gift.

—**Lana Vawser**
Author of *The Prophetic Voice of God, A Time to Selah,* and
I Hear the Lord say "New Era"
Lana Vawser Ministries

If you're yearning for revival, read this book! Bill Johnson has a way of illuminating the path to more of Jesus like few people I've ever encountered. In *Open Heavens* he shares profound insights from the scriptures and offers wise, practical instruction to help you carry revival into every area of life.

—**Eric Metaxas**
#1 *New York Times* bestselling author and host of
the nationally syndicated *Eric Metaxas Radio Show*

Read a book on revival, but only if the author has actually lived revival. Read a book on revival, but only if it removes the cobwebs that the enemy and bad preaching have placed on revival. Read a book on revival, but only if it not only makes revival doable but inevitable. Read this book.

—**Mario Murillo**
Bestselling author of *Vessels of Fire and Glory*

Open Heavens! Is it not what the depths of our soul longs for? We were created for revival. Newly born again, and filled with the Holy Spirit, I found myself searching for the "more" that Jesus offered His disciples. In an old missionary house in the Philippines, I found a book by Bill Johnson that imparted to me the gift of faith and helped me to see that *nothing* is impossible with God! Bill Johnson has once again written a book that is an invitation to us all, the saints, if we would so boldly accept. Bill has so thoughtfully shared *keys* that will give us access, each one purchased with risk, obedience, sacrifice, and trust. As I read *Open Heavens,* my heart burned within me, that we can really *know* and *follow* the person of Revival, Jesus! Let's go all in and partner with Him for revival, reformation, and renaissance!

—**Jessi Green**
Director of Saturate
Author of *Wildfires*

My friendship with Bill Johnson is one of my most treasured relationships and I am most excited about the subject matter of his new book, *Open Heavens.* And the timing could not be better, coming in the midst of an "evil day" on the face of the earth like the one Paul describes in Ephesians 6:13, because history tells us that every "evil day" has been followed by a great awakening. *Open Heavens* not only establishes that we, Jesus' Church—His Ekklesia—are designed by God for such a time as this, but it inspires and equips us to put His glory on display to turn the tide of evil and see God's will done on earth!

—**Dr. Ed Silvoso**
Author, *Ekklesia: Rediscovering God's Instrument for Global Transformation*
Founder, Transform Our World

OPEN
HEAVENS

DESTINY IMAGE BOOKS BY BILL JOHNSON

Rejoice Into Joy (with Beni)
How to Respond to Disaster
Experiencing Jesus Through Communion (with Beni)
Mornings and Evenings in His Presence (with Beni)
Resting Place
The King's Way of Life
The Way of Life
The Power of Communion (with Beni)
Is God Really Good?
God is Really Good
Encountering the Goodness of God
God is Good
Friendship with God
Hosting the Presence
Hosting the Presence Every Day
When Heaven Invades Earth
The Supernatural Power of a Transformed Mind
Strengthen Yourself in the Lord
Releasing the Spirit of Prophecy
Dreaming With God
Here Comes Heaven
Release the Power of Jesus
The Supernatural Ways of Royalty
Spiritual Java
A Life of Miracles
Center of the Universe
Dream Journal

OPEN HEAVENS

Position Yourself to Encounter the God of Revival

BILL JOHNSON

DEDICATION

I DEDICATE this book to Bethel Music, the 120 or so individuals who have committed themselves to excellence and beauty in the privilege of private and corporate worship. Over and over again you have touched the heart of God, revealed it in song, and made a mark in the course of Church history. I thank you. And to Brian and Jenn Johnson, and Joel Taylor and the countless others who serve behind the scenes, I thank you for leading this ministry in a way that is rooted in the local church, but always has the global Church in mind. For this and so many other reasons, I dedicate this book to you. And may the God of Revival, that you have written about so powerfully, visit us all once again and take us beyond our wildest dreams.

ACKNOWLEDGMENTS

I WANT to thank Larry Sparks for always believing in me as a writer. You've been a great encouragement and strength to me. I also want to thank my secretary Kelsey King and librarian Heidi Addy for doing research for me, and my PA Michael Van Tinteren for always helping me to succeed in whatever is on my plate at the moment. And to Pam Spinosi, you're an incredible help in refining the book through your edits and suggestions. It is better because of you.

DESTINY IMAGE® PUBLISHERS, INC.

P.O. Box 310, Shippensburg, PA 17257-0310

"Promoting Inspired Lives."

This book and all other Destiny Image and Destiny Image Fiction books are available at Christian bookstores and distributors worldwide.

Cover design by Christian Rafetto

For more information on foreign distributors, call 717-532-3040.

Reach us on the Internet: www.destinyimage.com.

ISBN 13 TP: 978-0-7684-5769-8

ISBN 13 eBook: 978-0-7684-5767-4

ISBN 13 HC: 978-0-7684-5766-7

ISBN 13 LP: 978-0-7684-5768-1

For Worldwide Distribution, Printed in the U.S.A.

1 2 3 4 5 6 7 8 / 25 24 23 22 21

CONTENTS

FOREWORD

by Daniel Kolenda

I SUPPOSE everyone can understand why you would never want to speak in a conference *after* Bill Johnson. He is a hard act to follow. But that was the situation I found myself in the first time we met. As I listened to him teach, I was awed by the wisdom in his words and the graceful way with which he related to each person. I fully expected that he would be on a plane that night flying on to his next gig. That's normal for conference speakers— especially those as highly sought after as Bill Johnson. To my surprise, the next day, as I began to preach, he was sitting there listening to me. Not only that, he was taking notes. Not only that, he was saying "amen" and encouraging me as I spoke. I'm quite certain there is nothing I said that was new to him. He did not know me and had no reason to be so gracious. But I saw in him the heart of a father—tender, genuine, wise and full of encouragement. I was struck by his humility, despite his tremendous stature in the Body of Christ. I have loved and honored him ever since.

This is what comes to mind when I think of Bill Johnson— he is a true father of the faith in our generation. More specifically, Bill is a true father of *revival* faith. Not only has he experienced revival in his own church and ministry for many years, but he has accumulated profound, biblical wisdom on how to sustain it. Yet he still hungers for more, longing for revival's fullest expressions to come to the Church and the world. That is what this book is about. It comes from Bill's longing for God's glory on earth as it is in Heaven. But it also comes from his highly seasoned place in the Body to father the next generation into glory.

Open Heavens is like a compressed computer file condensing massive amounts of data from many years of experience into tight, lucid prose. But once we open the file—once we take hold of Bill's simple yet profound writing on the subject—it yields a massive amount of spiritual insight for our future. Bill would never say he has arrived (a point he emphasizes in the book). But he is unusually qualified to speak with authority on the subject. And as a member of the next generation, I am grateful he has passed his knowledge to us.

One of the things that struck me most deeply in this book was how frankly Bill shared about the price he paid in pursuit of revival. His stories, laced with vulnerable candor, offer encouragement and practical advice on how to face the fear of man while fanning even the smallest flames into larger fires. Bill pulls no punches, frankly explaining that revival is costly, unpredictable, and sometimes unpopular. But he remains full of grace and tenderness without judgment. His personal illustrations are enormously relatable and will serve to inspire and empower. That's the beauty of this book. It is about something profoundly spiritual, yet it is practical and down to earth. Which is the point: "on *earth* as it is in Heaven." Through it all, and without denying the pain, Bill helps us see that the sacrifice for revival cannot be compared to its rewards.

As I see it, in this book, a father of revival faith gives my generation three gifts. The first is a clear *definition* of revival we can understand and pursue with passion. Second, a *burden* for *sustaining* revival. And finally, a clear vision of God's *goal* for revival: far-reaching impact on our cities and culture. He urges us not to pursue revival for its own sake, but for the glory of God. And God intends that glory to spill over from a revived Church into our city streets, societal structures, ethnic groups, spheres of influence, and art. Regardless of your particular eschatological views, we can all embrace Bill's main point. Revival is not just for the Church; it is for the world to see and experience the glory of God.

So, if you long for revival, or you desire to understand its purpose, read this book carefully. Receive its instruction with humility and its impartation with zeal. Let's take the torch from fathers like Bill Johnson so we can run our race even farther down the track—and then hand an even brighter torch to the generation after us.

—Daniel Kolenda
President of Christ for all Nations

FOREWORD

by Lou Engle

I'VE written many forewords in my life and it's been very fulfilling and a great joy to do so. I'm deeply honored to write this foreword for *Open Heavens* by the friend of God, and our friend, Bill Johnson. However, this one is somewhat challenging because Bill speaks of things of wonder, things which I've glimpsed and experienced in measure but yet still feel that I have only seen through a glass darkly. The apostle John wrote, *"That which was from the beginning, which we have heard, which we have seen with our eyes, which we have looked at and our hands have touched—this we proclaim concerning the Word of life"* (1 John 1:1 New International Version).

To me, Bill Johnson writes like John the Beloved. Both have seen something and touched something of the Heavenly Man that is not readily understood by the natural man, because these things are spiritually discerned. Both seek to frame heavenly concepts in thoughts and words that help us understand. I think both yearn that we "come up here" with them. In this book, Bill speaks of the things he's seen in revival and touched in personal encounter concerning the Word of Life. These are things that angels long to look into and, honestly, things that I long to look into.

Bill calls us inward into the inner recesses of our own hearts to be searched and known and to know the mind of Christ. He draws us upward into heavenly realities *"that eye has not seen and ear has not heard"* (1 Cor. 2:9). In reading, I find a reaching—a reaching up to touch the face of God and a pulling down of historic revival. I and the whole Body of Christ are deeply grateful for this man who calls us up to Heaven and reveals the Heaven that is already here on earth, the home of *revival* realities.

So, in some ways, I think that I should not call this a *Foreword*. I think I will say that I am writing an *Upward*. Why? Because I know that this book will, in itself, be a ladder upon which thousands will ascend into heavenly vision, heavenly understanding, and heavenly hunger, out of which Heaven will invade earth. It's an Upward because these writings, combining spiritual thoughts with spiritual words and describing real revival wonders, can break the gravitational pull on an earthbound humanity and give us wings to fly upward into face-to-face encounter personally and corporately in *revival!*

In January 2018, I spent a month in a very isolated area in the southernmost part of Hawaii. I was seeking God and fasting, except for a few of Hawaii's avocados and those little bananas that taste like candy. Now that's a heavenly fast! There, I was given a book called *Face to Face with God* by Bill Johnson, which I read while tucked away in the little prayer room of an Assembly of God church. Bill wrote of his personal journey of hunger in pursuit of a face-to-face encounter with God. He called that pursuit the "Ultimate Quest." I read of his months of ravenous desire and passionate pursuit of that face-to-face encounter. Then came the visitation for which he had longed—God came! He took him over, shook him, rearranged him. Maybe not unlike Jacob, who met face to face with God and ended up with a limp. I was torn up inside reading the story. I want such an encounter. At least I think so. Bill said this quest is an invitation to come and die. I don't think that I had ever thought that the ultimate quest was a face-to-face encounter with God. Oh yes, for 45 years I've certainly longed for spiritual encounter, but I didn't subscribe fully to the words of that great hymn:

> I ask no dream, no prophet ecstasies,
>
> no sudden rending of the veil of clay,
>
> no angel visitant, no opening skies;
>
> but take the dimness of my soul away.

No, I asked for dreams, for prophet ecstasies. But in some ways in my pursuit for God I had maybe given up an expectancy that I could actually see Jesus face to face or experience the kind of mighty baptism that I've read and heard about. Bill speaks of a dimension of God's face as His favor. I've known great favor but a face-to-face encounter being the ultimate quest? The book rocked my paradigm. I realized that much of my pursuit was more of what I would call the "vision quest." And oh, I have been on that quest: *"Show me the vision for my life. Unroll my scroll. Take my life and make it extraordinary. Send revival. Turn America back to God!"* Oh, what a wonderful, awesome quest, but not the ultimate quest. Show me Your face! Show me Your glory! That quest is meant to be answered. He comes where He is wanted! The book *Face to Face with God* should be read alongside *Open Heavens*. The first one is a pathway to a personal open Heaven encounter; this one, a commanding highway of destiny leading to true revival where the face of God shines upon and takes over a certain place, a certain city, or a certain nation.

In Genesis 28, we read that Jacob came to a *certain place*. He laid his head on a stone and dreamed of a stairway to Heaven where angels ascended and descended. There, the God of his fathers spoke. He called *the place* Bethel. I've been to Bethel Church in Redding, California where much of this book's description of revival takes place. I've been there several times, and often I've commented that there's no place, I think, that feels more like Heaven than Bethel. You see, the name Bethel is more than a cool Bible name attributed to a local church. In this case, Bethel is actually a description of what's really going on there. The Presence is there. Worship wings us to Heaven. There, testimonies abound of physical healings, healings of hearts, and healings of families and marriages.

I love in Genesis 28 where, over and over again, it speaks of Bethel as *the place*, a *certain place*. In other words, Bethel was a geographical location where the veil between Heaven and earth was thin. It was a landing spot for supernatural beings; it was literally a gate of Heaven, where Heaven and earth become one in dreams and visions and prophecy. There is a certain place in Redding that is like that. A visible cloud of glory at times can be seen there. Heaven and earth have collided. I'm sure Bethel is dissatisfied with what they have received. They rejoice in it, but long for more. This book is about that.

But what if every place was a certain place? What if every home had a thin veil? What if whole cities became Bethels? Well, this story is like that. The testimony of the Bethel revival, with its tests and trials, is really the trail to such heights. This book is not an easement of ease into some Promised Land. No, it is a call to holiness and prayer. This book reveals the ancient highways that our forefathers of revival walked on and beckon us, from the cloud, to walk again. It's a stony pathway of bloody feet, but oh, the glory.

Many reading such a book might say, "I've gotta move there!" And many have. I've thought about it myself. But maybe Heaven is where *you* live, and this book is *your* calling to touch that Heaven and reveal it in *your* certain place. Maybe it's better that a book would spread its seed wide and far that the hunger that possessed Bill and a small company of people might be a hunger that spreads, and is spreading, all over the world. Maybe every place will be a certain place, for is not this the promise? "Surely as I live, says the Lord, all the earth shall be filled with the glory of the Lord."

I believe this book will be a true instrument of revival—God's arrival, if you will. And men and women, churches, families, and communities will be the very ladders upon whom Heaven will ascend and descend. And there, a man running from his brother who wants to kill him will meet the God of Heaven, get a name change, and find his brother's face becomes the face of God.

Years ago I heard Dick Eastman, one of the great fathers of prayer in the earth, speak concerning how he carries a bag of seed on his shoulder. The seed is spiritual hunger. Everywhere he goes, he throws that seed and people become hungry for God. I think in this book Bill didn't just throw some seed out there, I think he threw the whole bag. And I, for one, want to grab as many kernels as I can.

—**Lou Engle**

PREFACE

WHEN Larry Sparks of Destiny Image Publishing asked me to write a book on revival, my heart leapt. Perhaps you'd understand it best if I said I was fearfully excited. Revival, and all that it is *unto*, is the burden and dream of my heart. It's why I'm alive. But it is also a very holy subject for me. It's not one I can afford to interject my own ideas into, without knowing I'm taking a great risk. There are very few things in life that are more terrifying than misrepresenting God. So, I offer this book to you as my best effort to touch and reveal the heart of God for planet Earth. And as always, I pray it is unto the glory of God.

Chapter One

OPEN HEAVENS: THE ULTIMATE REALITY

A true revival means nothing less than a revolution,
casting out the spirit of worldliness and selfishness, and
making God and His love triumph in the heart and life.
—ANDREW MURRAY

ONGOING revival is what we were born for. And the wonderful reality of ongoing revival is found in the presence of God. This is the great discovery, the great adventure found only in the experience of an open Heaven. Truly an open Heaven is our inheritance as believers.

The subject of an *open Heaven* appears as a promise of Scripture through the prophets, and is a mandated target in prayer. The open Heaven is where God's perfect world of beauty, order, and purpose fills this one so completely that it resembles Heaven in eternity, even though we're still here in time. Such a hope is not a lofty or baseless desire of the ignorant. Instead, it comes with the absolute conviction that this will happen, must happen, and in one sense is already within reach in measure. All increase in the Kingdom comes through the faithful stewardship of what has already been given, and we've been given so much.

Discovering and utilizing God's gift of an open Heaven must and will change everything.

All increase in the Kingdom comes through the faithful stewardship of what has already been given.

It's important to see that having an open Heaven is God's idea, God's will. As such, it is a prayer assignment for us. Isaiah declared it as a mandate in prayer in Isaiah 64:1. Jesus modeled it with the Spirit of God who rested upon Him in the form of a dove. And then Jesus also gave it to us as a prayer assignment with the phrase, *"on earth as it is in heaven."* (See Matthew 6:10.) His desire is to see His world influence all we are and all we do. The combination of prayer and obedience releases Heaven on earth/open Heavens. This reality is addressed in part by the thin veil that exists between the realm of eternity and time, between Heaven and earth, as is somehow accessible simply because He invites us to come.

SEEDS OF THOUGHT

As we open this book with such a unique subject, I want to plant a few seeds of thought through the following Scriptures. As our experiencing the open Heavens is very important to God, it must become increasingly important to us. While the Scriptures below are somewhat random, and in no particular order, each carries a thought that reveals God's heart for us in this present day of an *open Heaven*:

> *"Bring the whole tithe into the storehouse, so that there may be food in My house, and test Me now in this," says the Lord of hosts, "if I will not **open for you the windows of heaven** and pour out for you a blessing until it overflows"* (Malachi 3:10).

This passage from Malachi links the opening of the heavenly realm to the obedience of God's people. Interestingly, this manifestation of an open Heaven was in response to tithing and giving, which is the beginning place of good stewardship of money and resources. Jesus taught us later that faithfulness with money qualifies us for true riches. (See Luke 16:11.) The riches that Jesus was promising were not more money. His riches are the treasures of a heavenly realm, a realm that is available right now to permeate and influence our lives. I deal with this topic in more depth later.

> *After these things I looked, and behold, **a door standing open in heaven**, and the first voice which I had heard, like the sound of a trumpet speaking with me, said, "Come up here, and I will show you what must take place after these things." Immediately I was in the Spirit; and behold, a throne was standing in heaven, and One sitting on the throne* (Revelation 4:1-2).

I love this verse from Revelation because it speaks of God's desire for us, which is revealed in His invitation, *"Come up here."* That open Heaven was to enable John to see what must take place in the future. The point is, the open Heavens give us a unique vantage point from which to see.

Perception is clearer in the open Heaven realm. Everyone sees better and thinks clearer in that heavenlike environment.

> *In those days Jesus came from Nazareth in Galilee and was baptized by John in the Jordan. Immediately coming up out of the water,* **He saw the heavens opening***, and the Spirit like a dove descending upon Him; and a voice came out of the heavens: "You are My beloved Son, in You I am well-pleased"* (Mark 1:9-11).

This is one of the two primary verses we'll be looking at later in this chapter. The Heavens opened in response to Jesus' obedience in being baptized in water by John. It was a baptism of repentance. And Jesus had nothing to repent for. This was His intercessory role, as He identified with us and our need for the baptism of repentance.

Several other Scriptures shed light on the clarity that comes through the open Heavens:

> *But being full of the Holy Spirit, he gazed intently into heaven and saw the glory of God and Jesus standing at the right hand of God; and he said, "Behold,* **I see the heavens opened up** *and the Son of Man standing at the right hand of God"* (Acts 7:55-56).

This amazing account is of Stephen when he was martyred for his faith. Jesus, who is described as *"seated at the right hand of the Father,"* is seen standing in this story. Jesus stood to honor and welcome the first martyr of the Church. The point becomes clearer: Open Heavens give greater and clearer perception of the ultimate reality. And not seeing Jesus on the throne, and not living conscious of that reality, will always cause us to become more aware of inferior realities.

*But he became hungry and was desiring to eat; but while they were making preparations, he fell into a trance; and **he saw the sky opened up**, and an object like a great sheet coming down, lowered by four corners to the ground, and there were in it all kinds of four-footed animals and crawling creatures of the earth and birds of the air. A voice came to him, "Get up, Peter, kill and eat!"* (Acts 10:10-13).

Peter had a most unusual experience, spoken of in this passage. The Heavens opened so that he could see what he was to do: eat what he considered unclean food by Jewish law. The open Heaven was an experience that was far greater than having a subtle impression in the heart. God will sometimes increase the measure of our experience because He knows of our ability to forget or even discount what He has said. This command was much more than a dietary command. Through this, Peter would now gain additional insight to their much-needed theological adjustment to welcome Gentiles into the Church.

*Oh, that You would **rend the heavens** and come down, that the mountains might quake at Your presence* (Isaiah 64:1).

This will be the second passage that this chapter will be built around. It was both a prayer and a prophecy about an open Heaven. When He *rends* the Heavens, He comes.

VIOLENT ACTS OF GOD

There are many acts of God that we could consider violent. The Old Testament is especially attuned to such things—from the splitting of the

Red Sea, to the judgment that fell on Sodom and Gomorrah, to the lightnings and thundering on the mountain when Moses visited with God. All these, and so much more, could fall into that category. But there is one biblical violent act that surpasses them all for me. It was a New Testament experience at Jesus' water baptism.

Let's repeat the verse mentioned above:

> *In those days Jesus came from Nazareth in Galilee and was baptized by John in the Jordan. Immediately coming up out of the water,* **He saw the heavens opening,** *and the Spirit like a dove descending upon Him; and a voice came out of the heavens: "You are My beloved Son, in You I am well-pleased"* (Mark 1:9-11).

The primary purpose of this chapter is found in the phrase, *Heavens opening.* In the original language this word *opening* means "to rend," "to split," "to tear." It is a violent act.

The nature of this word used to describe Jesus' water baptism is further demonstrated when it appears in this verse from Matthew 27:51 at the death of Christ, *"And behold, the veil of the temple was **torn** in two from top to bottom; and the earth shook and the rocks were **split**."* This was a spiritually intense moment as the Son of God had just been crucified, and everything in time and eternity was affected. The veil in the temple was *torn* from top to bottom, from God's side to ours. He is the one who destroyed what separates us from Him (this was accomplished through the blood sacrifice of the Lamb of God) and demonstrated it in the tearing of the veil.

The second word highlighted in this verse is the word *split*. The word used for both *torn* and *split* is the same word used in Jesus' water baptism. It carries with it an even greater display of violence, in that along with a veil being torn, big boulders were simply *torn in two*. Rocks! They were torn apart. By the nature of the word used, we can see that the open Heaven above Jesus in His baptism was not a simple parting of clouds. The very fact that this was a violent act implies there was resistance, or an already existent power in place. Spiritual darkness needed to be broken. I believe it was a demonic realm that worked to keep people in spiritual blindness. But Jesus was and is the light that came to enlighten every person born into the world (see John 1:9). And at His water baptism, the Heavens were opened (torn open!), and the Holy Spirit came down. Think of it: The wonderful Holy Spirit came down, through the open Heavens, and rested upon Jesus. And He never left Him.

In summary, an open Heaven is all about the presence of God: seeing, understanding, encountering, and perceiving realities that circumstances would deny, participating in greater realities, and partnering with Him to see the abundance of His world come and fill ours.

GOD ANSWERS PRAYER

The second verse I'd like to highlight from the list above is from Isaiah 64:1, "*Oh, that You would **rend the heavens** and come down, that the mountains might quake at Your presence.*" We are so accustomed to reading prophecies that still need fulfillment that we all too often live unaware of what has already been accomplished. These fulfilled promises enable us to fulfill our assignment and destiny. And this verse is, for me, a most important promise to remember.

In the Mark 1 account of Jesus' water baptism, we see God fulfill the prophecy, and at the same time answer the intercessory prayer of Isaiah.

"Rend the heavens and come down." That is word for word what happened in this moment. The obedience of Jesus brought about an open Heaven, through which the Spirit of God came down and rested upon Him. It was torn open, and He came, which was essential in that it was the Holy Spirit who enabled Jesus to see and do what the Father was doing. He was central to all that Jesus was assigned to do.

We function with the realization that there are at least three realms of Heaven mentioned in Scripture. I mention this point as it is vital to remember that the powers of darkness could never block or interrupt what God does in Heaven, which is the realm of His undisturbed rule. While He is certainly Lord over all, He has allowed the influence of humanity to play a role in our world. He is in charge but has chosen not to control the decisions we make.

- *First Heaven:* That is the realm we live in day to day. It is all that is earthly and seen with the natural eye.

- *Second Heaven:* That is the realm of angels and demons. It is spiritual/unseen with the natural eye, but is not the realm of Heaven itself.

- *Third Heaven:* That is the realm of Heaven itself, where the throne of God is. Everything in that realm is perfect and wonderful under His dominion and rule. Righteousness, peace, and joy are prevailing influences as all that exists finds its identity and fulfillment in His design.

An open Heavens makes what exists in the perfect, God realm available to influence and shape the first Heaven, where we live, without the interference from the second realm.

CONFLICTING REALITIES

The Holy Spirit, who lives in every believer, came through an open Heaven, the same way as happened with Jesus. James speaks of the Father and His heart for the Holy Spirit: *"He jealously desires the Spirit which He has made to dwell in us"* (James 4:5). So, let's look at the greater reality: The Holy Spirit came to us through an open Heaven. And it's the Father who longs for fellowship with the Spirit who dwells in us. My question is this: What power of darkness can block the fellowship of the Father with the Spirit? None. Absolutely none. The implication is that as believers, we live under an open Heaven. Our problem is not that we need God to do something in addition to what's already happened; our problem is that we live unaware of what He has already done for us, and how He has designed us to live as a result.

There is no battle between God and satan.

God is infinite power.

We live in a spiritual world with light and darkness, good and evil, and spiritual forces of wickedness that work to interfere with what God is saying and doing. But let me make something very clear—there is no battle between God and satan. God is infinite power. The devil is created and extremely limited, especially as compared to God Himself. The picture that some have created of this great war between God and the devil is a joke. A very, very sad joke. It wouldn't be a contest in the least. The war was between the devil and those created in the image of God: humanity. When we gave up our right and responsibility through sin, Jesus became a man and thoroughly beat the devil through His death and resurrection in our place. His victory became our victory. So, now, in His name we have the right and responsibility to trample the powers of darkness and put on display the beauty of God's original plan: defeat the powers of darkness through those made in His image.

Our problem lies in our tendency to live aware of what the devil has done or is doing and then react to it. Jesus, on the other hand, lived in response to the Father. He set the pattern that we can and must follow. Secondly, we always reflect the nature of the world we are most aware of. If the world around us is one of chaos, confusion, sin, and unbelief, and that reality is what has captured our attention, it will show on our countenance. On the other hand, if we live aware of the open Heaven He has given us access to, we will in like manner reflect the nature of that world through our countenance. I believe the prayer for the favor of God's countenance upon us is actually a prayer to become more aware of His world than any other. (See Psalm 67:1 and Numbers 6:24-26.) This is the blessed life of a believer.

WHO IS WAITING ON WHOM?

We often wait for God to act, when He, in fact, is waiting for us to believe His Word and live fully in what He has provided for us. He waits for us to act out of a faith in what He has accomplished and promised. Perhaps it was for this reason He instructs to *"keep seeking the things above, where Christ is, seated at the right hand of God"* (Col 3:1). A mind set on things above, where Christ is seated, testifies of an open Heaven. It's what Stephen saw in his open Heaven experience in Acts 7:55-56; it was marked by the person of Jesus Christ and the throne of God. We are commanded to set our minds on this superior reality because that act alone enables us to see what we've set our eyes to see, all in obedience to Him. Without the awareness of the open Heaven, we will live in an inferior way to His design and plan for our lives.

We often wait for God to act, when He in fact is waiting for us to believe His Word and live fully in what He has provided for us.

REVIVAL AND THE OPEN HEAVEN

The day of Pentecost was a day of open Heaven experiences. Their intoxication is not a surprise for anyone who has experienced His overwhelming presence. It truly is intoxicating. I remind you that Paul taught us, *"And do not get drunk with wine, for that is dissipation, but be filled with the Spirit"* (Eph. 5:18). The comparison, while offensive to some, is understandable to those who have been overwhelmed by His manifest presence.

Whenever the Holy Spirit is poured out upon people, it is the flashpoint of revival. He carries the realm of Heaven and is Himself the expression of that world here on earth. That moment of outpouring is what ignites us into our divine purpose—acquainting us with a burning found only in His presence.

> ## Whenever the Holy Spirit is poured out upon people, it is the flashpoint of revival.

Revivals are the best and most glorious state of the church this side of Heaven itself.[1]

That statement really is the ultimate lifestyle for the Church here on earth. Revival is the reality of Heaven revealed through His manifest presence. Heaven, revealed in revival, is more clearly made known in the here and now.

ETERNITY NOW

Heaven is what we were born for. The reality of His rule is the most wonderful discovery available to us, as it is all found in our discovery of the ruler. In other words, we encounter His manifest presence, and everything changes. This is the life of those who truly live in an open Heaven, as it is all about Him. Revival then becomes a way of life.

NOTES

1. Simeon W. Harkey, *The Church's Best State or Constant Revivals of Religion* (Sydney: Wentworth Press, 2019), 78.

Chapter Two

MY PERSONAL JOURNEY

*Revival is God revealing Himself to men in
awesome holiness and irresistible power.*
—ARTHUR WALLIS

WHEN I said yes to Jesus, it was not partial or conditional. I don't care for the bumper sticker of the '70s, "Try Jesus." As Winkie Pratney, the great teacher and friend from New Zealand, would tell us, "Jesus is not on trial. We are." My *yes* was a complete abandonment of my goals, ambitions, possessions and rights. All just to follow Him. It wasn't careless, nor was it casual. Now I can see that He gave me grace for that moment as His absolute *yes* for me became my absolute *yes* for Him.

It has been close to 50 years since I prayed the scary prayer, "God you can have everything." While I was raised in church and grew up with an awareness of God and His love for me, what God was asking from me was different from what I was accustomed to. I knew this was it, never to be brought up for renegotiation.

This journey has been more fulfilling and rewarding than I thought possible. It has also been costly in ways that never crossed my mind. But my choice to give all and do all was made a long time ago for the One who gave it all for me.

It's important to know that the price we pay is never greater than the blessings we receive. His Kingdom doesn't work that way. It would be foolish to plant one kernel of corn expecting to harvest only one kernel in return. Not even nature allows for that kind of thinking. And so, I try to live aware that every loss is temporary and every blessing is eternal.

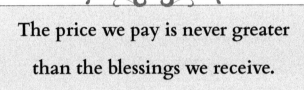

The price we pay is never greater

than the blessings we receive.

WHAT I HAVE SEEN

I must admit I have seen more than I ever thought I would. None of it has been earned. And even when He responded to great faith on my part; faith was His gift to me. All is by grace. Yet in another sense, I've seen what is available in Christ, and it feels like I'm just getting started. I have been apprehended by God for a purpose: revival—the outlandish move of the Holy Spirit. And in response, I am apprehending that purpose through the faith that comes from surrender.

THE INVITATION TO SPEAK

In December of 1995, I was invited to speak at Bethel Church, the place where Beni and I have been for the last 25 years. This is the church family that sent us out 17 years earlier to pastor the people of Mountain Chapel in Weaverville, California. Bethel was its mother church.

The leadership from Bethel visited Mountain Chapel and had seen the move of God we were experiencing. As their pastor had just left, they asked me to come back and take his place. I came to speak on that December Sunday morning so the people could see what they would be getting if I were brought in. During my message, I told them, "I was born for revival, and it's not negotiable. Revivals are very messy. If you don't want that, you don't want me." The overwhelming response was *yes*! They were hungry and hoped they would see a great move of God in this next season.

My comment on revival not being negotiable wasn't as rude as it looks in print. But neither was it a hyped statement trying to persuade anyone that I was the one they wanted. We were experiencing an amazing move of God in Weaverville, and I felt honored to be where God was having His way. A move to a bigger church was not important to me, nor did I necessarily consider it a promotion. All I wanted was to be a part of something that no person could take credit for. My comment was both gut-level honesty and a warning of pending challenges if they said yes. I knew that God showing up in unexpected ways would be an expensive endeavor for all of us.

Revival is a continuous yielding to the Holy Spirit. This is the purpose for which I am alive. My lifelong journey is to learn His ways and navigate the direction of my life in response.

Revival is a continuous yielding to the Holy Spirit. This is the purpose for which I am alive.

Yielding is essential for great faith. But great faith is anything but passive. Little gets done through passive anything. Mountains are moved through the aggressive actions that prove faith's existence. No amount of effort can bring about the miracle of God. It is not the product of our efforts or personal strength. Faith comes through surrender, not striving. But it must be displayed through actions.

The absolute *yes* from this church family reveals that the cry for revival is deeply embedded in the hearts of God's people. While I know our definitions vary in different parts of the Body of Christ, we know instinctively revival is the will of God because in revival *God has His way*.

GROOMED FOR REVIVAL

Twenty-five years earlier, I was in the youth group at this same church. My dad was the pastor, and Chip Worthington was the youth pastor. My dad eventually led this church into a wonderful move of God. Both the Jesus People Movement and the Charismatic Renewal were important expressions of who we were as a church family. But in 1970 we had the beginning of the birth pangs. I love the *birth pang* analogy, as it reminds us of this reality: "Birth pangs don't bring the baby. It's the baby that brings the birth pangs." The ache in our hearts was in measure the indication that God had something wonderful planned for us. Our ache was the sign that what God had promised was on the way. It was a seed planted in our hearts and watered by Mario Murillo and many other Charismatic leaders. But it would be a year or so before a major breakthrough came.

I was around 19 at this time, and became immersed in Mario's teachings as well as those of Winkie Pratney and our youth pastor Chip Worthington. They spoke often of this thing called "revival," telling us the stories from history when God showed up in unusual and powerful ways to change individuals, the Church, and ultimately the world. It became clear to me that I had never seen one before, and the thing I grew up hearing was revival actually wasn't. There's no such thing as a week of revival meetings. Wildfire can't be corralled into a seven-day period of time. We can have special meetings during that time, even powerful meetings, but not revival. Ultimately, revival is all-consuming, whether it is with one person carrying the fire of His presence, a church, or an entire movement. Little else matters during these times.

I am forever indebted to Chip and his wife Linda for so much. Chip fed me with a constant flow of books, especially the classics on prayer, like those by Andrew Murry, Praying Hyde, Norman Grubb, R. A. Torrey, and many more. This non-reader became a reader. I found food for my soul that I had never encountered before. I was hooked. In the natural realm we get hungry by not eating. But in the Kingdom, we get hungry by eating. This was certainly the newfound reality for me.

PRAYER WAS KEY

Early in my journey, in everything I heard and read, the one constant was that *revival comes through prayer*. A lot of it. For a young man who had never prayed much beyond the blessings for family and food, this was a whole new thing. I started to get up early and go to bed late, having extensive times of prayer. It was good, and it was a beginning. Yet, I have to admit that most of my prayers were about me. But they were still prayed with great sincerity.

Knowing that holiness was important to God was probably the main reason my prayers were focused so heavily on me. I was prone to make the focus all about my unworthiness and impurity. These are spiritually sneaky ways of staying self-focused. I even confessed sins that I never committed, just in case they had entered my mind. It seems silly now, but hungry people are known to do desperate things. It was time with God nonetheless, and He treasured it as it was honest and my real effort to live in surrender to Him even though I remained the primary focus. Besides, all two-year-olds think the world rotates around them. I'm pretty sure that was my spiritual age.

Chip would call random prayer meetings, always late at night, and always for a great move of God. I remember one night around 30 of us went about 10 miles out of town to a lake called Whiskeytown Lake. It was around midnight. We tried to find an isolated area that was both open and level enough for us to stand in a big circle to worship God and pray. We finally found the ideal place, in the dark, mind you. I remember it as though it was yesterday. We sang the song, "Oh, How I Love Jesus!" over and over again, with hands raised high. We thought we had that whole part of the lake to ourselves as there were no campfires or any other signs of life. What we didn't know is that this area was party central, and there were people getting drunk all around us at the campsites hidden by the manzanita bushes and pine trees. Soon people began to leave their party and come and stand around us, a group of singing young people. One by one someone from our group would step back from the circle to talk and pray with anyone who came out of the bushes. I remember how a guy I talked with was so deeply moved that he took his can of beer and began to pour it out on the ground as I shared the love of God with him. Apparently, his appetite was changing for a drink of the water from which you will never thirst again. This was one of those moments when God gave His own altar call, and people came to see our love for God, hoping to find a similar place of peace for themselves. It was later that I read the statement by John Wesley, "Light yourself on fire with passion, and people will come from miles to watch you burn." That's exactly what happened—simple, unadulterated love for Jesus. Many lives were touched that night. It was beautiful.

Dick Eastman, a true prophet of prayer, called for an all-night prayer gathering at a Christian campground. It was my first time for an all-nighter, but certainly not my last. Dick was known as a man of prayer and a teacher of prayer, leading countless numbers of people into a place of strength in their intercessory call. This particular gathering of young people will always stand out to me, as this was the first time I heard the voice of God so clearly. And He spoke to me about my life. This happened when I went into a side room next to the corporate meeting room just so I could rest. When I lay down, He spoke. The manner in which He spoke was to set a standard that would long impact how He would deal with me in the years to come. It wasn't audible, but it was that clear. It's a great mystery to me how He can be so loud, yet make no sound. He said, "If you will stay out of my way, I will use you in no small way." That was it. No more, no less. It stood out to me for so many reasons. But one was that I don't even think with those kinds of words —*no small way*. If I had come up with such a statement, I would have said, *in a big way*. Secondly, it was my introduction to the sovereignty of God. I couldn't bring about what God had planned, but I could interfere. Anyway, the encounter deeply impacted me. It was years before I told anyone about that moment. I've never written about it until now.

All night prayer meetings became more common. Sometimes they were organized by our leaders, and sometimes we did them on our own. We prayed, knowing that something good would happen as a result. Sometimes the *good that happened* was immediate, but it was often an investment into our future.

Another such prayer meeting happened even later at night. Again, it was probably another 30 people or so, and this time it took place around 2 a.m., at a small, 24-hour grocery store. We chose that place because their parking lot had become the main location in town to buy illegal drugs. Dealers would linger there for a sale, or the pay phone would be used, and the dealer would come with the goods. Their activities were rather brazen and in the open. This was during the hippie era, so there were long-haired, young people all over this establishment. As we gathered in the parking lot to pray, the manager came out and mocked us with laughter. It was too late for any crowds to be there. If ever I heard demonic laughter, it was then. Soon the police came. The officer asked Chip what we were doing. He said, "We're praying for you." The officer thanked him and asked him to keep it up and then left. We did. But something happened that night that I'll never forget. The drug dealing stopped at that location from that night on. It completely stopped. I drove by the store the next night, and there was no crowd lingering, which was unheard of. This was also confirmed by a friend of mine who was a drug user at that time. After his conversion to Christ, we were talking about how he came to meet Jesus. He mentioned how he used to buy drugs at that same grocery store. But when he went there to buy his drugs on this particular Saturday night, as he had apparently done many times before, there was no one there. He could never figure how or why the drug dealers suddenly stopped using this location. There didn't seem to be any logical explanation. We compared notes and found it was following our prayer meeting. Prayer matters. It makes a difference. But if prayers don't move us, they won't move Him.

Interestingly, this same man began to lead prayer teams in various locations around our city in the years that followed. They would sense God directing them to pray for a particular business known for sin and depravity. For what it's worth, they were not prayers for judgment. We simply prayed for God to come and have His way. On most, if not all, occasions those businesses closed down quickly after such prayers. I have a big place in my heart for businesses. They are the bedrock of our communities. And I love supporting them. But a business whose livelihood depends on promoting evil is another matter altogether. It's not my call. God knows. And it's an amazing journey to see what has to leave when His manifest presence comes.

MIRACLES, TOO

Although I believed in God's power to heal, I had not seen much. During this time, the youth group had twin girls who had come to Christ. They both had very severe epilepsy. We prayed, and they were both healed. On their own they stopped all medication, which we found out later was quite dangerous because of their unusually high dosage. But there were no effects at all. Not only that, when the mother found out what they had done, she panicked and took them to the doctor. He verified what had happened and warned the mother that if they started that level of medication again, they could die.

Needless to say, I began to burn for revival. I became hungry. I prayed for it, declared my desire for it, and went anywhere I thought it might be possible to see it, all while not really knowing what it was. But I knew enough to know it was good, and it was God. That's all I needed to know in order to pursue it. And so, I did, day and night.

I want to reprint here a passage from my book, *When Heaven Invades Earth,* in which I share the moment all my prayers reached a tipping point.

GLORIOUS BUT NOT PLEASANT

In my personal quest for increased power and anointing in my ministry, I have traveled to many cities, including

Toronto. God has used my experiences in such places to set me up for life-changing encounters at home.

Once in the middle of the night, God came in answer to my prayer for more of Him, yet not in a way I had expected. I went from a dead sleep to being wide-awake in a moment. Unexplainable power began to pulsate through my body, seemingly just shy of electrocution. It was as though I had been plugged into a wall socket with a thousand volts of electricity flowing through my body. My arms and legs shot out in silent explosions as if something was released through my hands and feet. The more I tried to stop it, the worse it got.

I soon discovered that this was not a wrestling match I was going to win. I heard no voice, nor did I have any visions. This was simply the most overwhelming experience of my life. It was raw power...*it* was God. He came in response to a prayer I had been praying for months—*God, I must have more of you at any cost!*

The evening before was glorious. We were having meetings with a good friend and prophet, Dick Joyce. The year was 1995. At the end of the meeting, I prayed for a friend who was having difficulty experiencing God's presence. I told him that I felt God was going to surprise him with an encounter that could come in the middle of the day, or even at 3 a.m. When the power fell on me that night, I looked at the clock. It was 3 a.m., exactly. I knew I had been set up.

For months I had been asking God to give me more of Him. I wasn't sure of the correct way to pray, nor did I understand the doctrine behind my request. All I knew was I was hungry for God. It had been my constant cry day and night.

This divine moment was glorious, but not pleasant. At first, I was embarrassed, even though I was the only one who knew I was in that condition. As I lay there, I had a mental picture of me standing before my congregation, preaching the Word as I loved to do. But I saw myself with my arms and legs flailing about as though I had serious physical problems. The scene changed—I was walking down the main street of our town, in front of my favorite restaurant, again arms and legs moving about without control.

I didn't know of anyone who would believe that this was from God. I recalled Jacob and his encounter with the angel of the Lord. He limped for the rest of His life. And then there was Mary, the mother of Jesus. She had an experience with God that not even her fiancé believed, although a visit from an angel helped to change his mind. As a result, she bore the Christ-child...and then bore a stigma for the remainder of her days as *the mother of the illegitimate child.* It was becoming clear; the favor of God sometimes looks different from the perspective of earth than from heaven. My request for more of God carried a price.

Tears began to soak my pillowcase as I remembered the prayers of the previous months and contrasted them with the scenes that just passed through my mind. At the forefront was the realization that God wanted to make an exchange—His increased presence for my dignity. It's difficult to explain how you know the purpose of such an encounter. All I can say is you just *know.* You know His purpose so clearly that every other reality fades into the shadows, as God puts His finger on the one thing that matters to Him.

In the midst of the tears came a point of no return. I gladly yielded, crying, *More, God. More! I must have more of You at any cost! If I lose respectability and get You in the exchange, I'll gladly make that trade. Just give me more of You!*

The power surges didn't stop. They continued throughout the night, with me weeping and praying, *More Lord, more, please give me more of You.* It all stopped at 6:38 a.m., at which time I got out of bed completely refreshed. This experience continued the following two nights, beginning moments after getting into bed.[1]

HE CAME TO BETHEL IN POWER!

Beni and I accepted the invitation to be the new senior pastors of Bethel Church and began serving in that capacity in February of 1996. They were a wonderful group of believers, with an amazing pastoral team, which I inherited from the previous pastor. On one of the first Sunday nights, I invited the whole church up to the front of the sanctuary. I wanted us to pray together. The church was thankful that we had come to be their pastors, but they were also very tired. Their previous pastor, Ray Larson, was a wonderful man and personal friend. He had transitioned around eight months earlier. They had been searching for his replacement during this time and had become weary in doing so. As hundreds of people gathered around the front of the auditorium, Beni and I simply stood together on the platform and invited the Holy Spirit to come. You could argue the case that He was already there, which would be biblically accurate. We gathered in His name and He was present. But there are dimensions and levels of His presence that a doctrine won't satisfy, any more than a marriage license can satisfy the longing we have for relationship with our spouse. In the same way that a marriage license makes a relationship possible, so the doctrine invites us to experience Him in a way that is transformative. He is to be encountered, known, and enjoyed. Plus, there is always more.

We shared a genuine ache in our hearts for the MORE of God to fill our lives and that place. As I lifted up my voice, He came. The power of God fell in the room that night. It was beautiful. But He came noticeably on only one person. I'm not saying this woman was the only one touched by God, as He moves in subtle ways as well as in the overtly powerful demonstrations. But in this case His obvious manifestation of power fell on one person only, out of the hundreds present. She fell to the ground under the weighty presence of God, trembling under His power. Beni and I looked at each other and said, "We've got it. It is now unstoppable!" Metaphorically speaking this was the *"cloud the size of a man's hand,"* which was a moment given to Elijah when he was praying for rain. The small sign from God was all he needed to know that rain was at hand, and he ran for cover as a result. (See 1 Kings 18:44.) In the days that followed, we experienced the ever-increasing downpour we had only read about in history books on revival. And through those stories of old, this had become our dream. It should be normal for us to dream and explore what might be possible in our lifetimes.

I knew that what God was doing in the earth would now be unstoppable, as it was now in the church family, not just the leadership team. And as much as I try to get rid of that notion that only pastoral staff members are ministers, there's a residue in people's thinking. Anyway, once the power of the Holy Spirit fell upon this one woman, it was like the leaven that gets kneaded into dough. Once it's in, it can't be removed. We knew that the impact of this move of God would become measurable in time. And it was.

It should be normal for us to dream and explore what might be possible in our lifetimes.

As I consider that moment which became so formative in giving place to God's activities among us, I remember the story of Evan Roberts in one of my favorite revivals of all time: The Welsh Revival of 1904 and 1905. In the first meeting, the pastor/vicar allowed Evan to speak to anyone who wanted to stay after the main meeting. In this after-glow gathering, Evan challenged those present to give their all to Jesus. The 16 adults present all responded. By the end of the week, he had the public confession of faith in Jesus from a total of 65 people. The next day he wrote to the editor of the newspaper saying, "We are on the eve of a great and grand Revival, the greatest Wales has ever seen.² The 65 surrendered believers were his *"cloud, the size of a man's hand."* It wasn't the number of people that mattered. It was the quality of their *yes*. And much like the mustard seed that grows into a large plant or the loaves and fishes multiplied to feed a multitude, so it is with anything we give to Jesus in surrender. It is limitless in its inherent potential through the completeness of our *yes*.

Many people abort what God has given them because it didn't come to them fully developed. I hear from so many who look at what God is doing and say, "This isn't revival" as though they speak with utmost discernment and maturity. It saddens me, really. Nothing of significance grows when we verbally abuse or discredit any of the seemingly small gifts of God. The Scripture is clear about not despising small beginnings. Their criticisms become self-fulfilling prophecies in that those subtle touches of God seldom grow into all that God intended. And the critic lives with the false sense of *being right* through their discernment. It is usually not discernment. It is unbelief. Their words are destructive to the work of God. Perhaps this is why God silenced Zacharias for nine months while his son, John, was growing in the womb. His words and questions were of unbelief, not curiosity, and they were very destructive in nature.

We are heirs and stewards of life and death according to Paul in First Corinthians 3:22. This truth connects powerfully to what is revealed in the book of wisdom, Proverbs 18:21: "Death and life are in the power of the tongue." That wasn't made up by any group, or denomination. God said it. We must take heed and be careful for what comes out of our mouths regarding anything that God does or gives. I've grieved as I've watched fellow believers criticize what God gave them because it wasn't what they expected or wanted. If I give two gifts to each of my children, one expensive and one inexpensive, I will not be happy with them if they celebrate the expensive gift and leave the other under their chair. And yet believers do that all the time. They'll say something like, "I'm pursuing being used by God in prophecy. Tongues is a lesser gift; therefore, I'll give my attention to what God values most." That is an abuse of Scripture and ignores the fact that God only does wonderous things. Praying in tongues is a most special gift as it is the only one of the nine listed that is specifically to be used for our edification. Plus, it enables us to speak directly to God from our spiritual man, with no soulish interference. (See First Corinthians 14:2.) Our treatment of the gifts of the Holy Spirit runs an interesting parallel course to our readiness to live in the anointing for revival.

Most of the time our greatest prayers are answered in seed form to give us the chance to grow in our ability to steward the answer as it comes in fullness. This sets the stage for the larger answer. In other words, instead of God giving them an oak tree, He gives them an acorn. Faith sees there's an oak tree in the acorn. And there's an unlimited number of acorns in the oak tree. The point is we must see the potential in the answer He gives us, or we'll not take care of the answer properly.

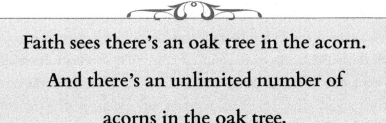

> **Faith sees there's an oak tree in the acorn. And there's an unlimited number of acorns in the oak tree.**

In the months that followed, I began to see things happen that I had hungered for, for as long as I could remember. I had always read about the God who healed and set free, but had never seen it on a large scale.

THANKFUL, BUT NOT SATISFIED

When you start to see things you've only heard about by reading of revivals in Church history stories, or from the stories found on the pages of Scripture, it's almost too much to handle. Thankfulness erupts! But there is also a sobering awareness that this precious gift from God must not be mishandled, as it is the evidence that represents and reveals His heart the most. We are stewards. But as I mentioned earlier, one of the outcomes of *eating* in the Kingdom is greater hunger. It is no wonder that participating in the outpourings of the Holy Spirit actually creates an even greater hunger for the same—outpourings of the Holy Spirit. We are daily being introduced to a Kingdom without limits or end.

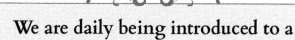

We are daily being introduced to a Kingdom without limits or end.

NOTES

1. Bill Johnson, *When Heaven Invades Earth*. (Shippensburg, PA: Destiny Image Publishers, 2005), Chapter 10.

2. Phillips, *Evan Roberts,* 190. Letter from Evan Roberts to Elsie Phillips, November 5, 1904.

Chapter Three

WINE IN
THE CLUSTER

If you want to go fast, go alone.
But if you want to go far, go together.
—AFRICAN PROVERB

WHAT often starts with one person crying out to God in private soon moves to a small group of trusted friends. It is in that nucleus that dramatic increase happens. Isaiah saw this when he said, *"The new wine is found in the cluster"* (Isa. 65:8). Likened unto the new wine, the outpouring of the Spirit is found when there is a unified gathering together, as in *the cluster.* We see it with the 120 believers in the upper room of Acts 2:1. They were in perfect unity. I'm not saying that an individual cannot experience revival. I believe it often starts with one. But healthy fires always spread.

One of the first promises God gave me when I became a pastor was from Psalm 118:7, *"The Lord is for me among those who help me."* Basically, His promise to me was that while there might be opposition, He would support me through those He had put in my life to help. It became obvious early on that I would live and thrive only in the midst of a team of friends. And so it has been.

Healthy fires always spread.

Having said that, I inherited a wonderful staff from the previous pastor when I came to Bethel. He was a great man, who knew how to build a team. While it is customary for a new pastor to release the previous staff and bring in his own, I kept them all. They served and helped me in the most admirable way. Looking back, I can see that that was one of the smartest things I've ever done. I couldn't have found a better group of leaders to help me serve the Bethel family. They had history with the people as well as the wisdom and devotion needed to go further. Plus, they had that X-factor: a hunger for all that God was doing.

They wanted to help me lead this church family by learning how to navigate life in the midst of this new outpouring. But they were also wise enough to know they were not equipped to do so in the way that was needed. Alan Ray, one of the key pastors who had been at Bethel the longest, asked me if it might be possible to have a private meeting with our pastors where they could be in a receive mode, instead of feeling the need to lead. If they were also touched by the power of God in a deeply personal way, they could better help me lead. You only need to be a step ahead of the others to lead effectively.

We scheduled a meeting at the home of one of the pastors. I then invited two ministry teams to come and help us: one from Weaverville, the other from Hayfork, (two small mountain communities). They came and served with great humility. The power of God came upon us in such an extraordinary way, it started the slow burn of His presence and power in the church staff.

That meeting worked so well I thought it wise to do the same with our whole leadership team, to help us all be on the same page. I called for a meeting with about 100 leaders. We met in an upper room in our facilities. I did as I had done a number of times before by talking for a few minutes on what God was doing and then inviting the Holy Spirit to come. He did, once again. This time was quite unusual in that many were touched powerfully, but there was a notable impact on one man named Cal Pierce.

What made Cal's encounter so unusual was that he did not like what was happening in the church and was planning his exodus. He had been there 25 years, so it was no small matter. But his mind was made up, and his exit strategy was in place. To his credit, he also knew as a church board member what responsibility was, so he came to the meeting I asked all our leaders to attend. Cal was not hungry and certainly not impressed with what was happening in the church through my leadership. Like many others, he was leaving. But that night I watched as God selected him. God chose to touch this man who had little to no interest in this move of the Holy Spirit. If ever I've seen God sovereignly choose someone, it was that night. In about an hour's time he went from complacent to passionate, from being distant to being in the center of it all, and from an opponent to the move of God, to a promoter and facilitator. This was an extraordinary miracle, one of the greatest I had seen up until that time.

Following that night, Cal cared about little else than what God was saying and doing. His heart burned in ways I've seen few people burn. He had a special passion for healing and took it on as a special assignment, knowing it was central to the Gospel of the Kingdom. I remember one night in particular. We were having a special conference, which was a wonderful way for us to serve the Body of Christ at large. A woman in attendance was dancing in worship at the back of the sanctuary. Something happened where she fell and broke her foot. She was also an emergency room nurse at a local hospital and was familiar with her injury. The bone protruded away from the foot in a way that was visible to all. But it wasn't a compound fracture where the bone pierced through the skin. She asked several people if they believed God would heal her if they prayed. Each of them, including one of the speakers, said he'd be glad to pray for her. She responded, "You're not the one." She asked Cal the same question, "Do you believe my foot will be healed if you pray?" He said, "Yes!" She said, "You're the one." He prayed, and they watched the bone come back into place. The pain left, and she was completely healed. That man, Cal Pierce, only weeks earlier wanted to leave the church. And then he was apprehended by the Sovereign One, who basically said, "I have need of you." Today Cal heads up The International Healing Rooms, which has hundreds of healing room ministries all around the world.

SIGNS THAT MAKE YOU WONDER

One of the most tragic things to happen to those who are born again is to lose the wonder of God and the wonder of our salvation. Sadly, wonder has become an unnecessary part of many people's lives. We've been born again by the same Spirit that raised Christ from the dead, which introduced us to a Kingdom lifestyle that is one ongoing adventure. The absence of the recognized presence of God among us is at the root. Christian activities, no matter how wonderful they are, will never satisfy the cry of the heart for Him.

What we started to experience in those early years was the overwhelming presence of God in our gatherings. We always had a plan in place for the meeting, but were even more delighted whenever He interrupted our plans with one of His own. I remember one Sunday morning in particular when my son Brian played one or two chords on his guitar, and the glory came into the room. Literally. We were overwhelmed by God. It was around 40 minutes later that we sang our first song. An amazing part of these kinds of invasions is that we lose track of time. In other words, 40 minutes without a clear direction except the awe of God didn't make people restless for what would happen next.

Christian activities, no matter how wonderful they are, will never satisfy the cry of the heart for Him.

It is also interesting to note that this manifestation of presence was not recognized by everyone. Those who had built an antagonism in their hearts had a harder time discerning what was happening. Jacob's story is particularly dear to me in that he lay down to sleep and had a dream. When he woke up, he stated, *"Surely the Lord is in this place, and I did not know it."* (Gen. 26:16). We all sometimes need help recognizing the moment we are in. God can be at hand, but our own issues make us blind to the single reality in our lives. I have seen my share of meetings where the power and presence of God were unmistakable yet unrecognized by some. One person has a life-changing experience, and next to them is someone who can hardly wait to get home to eat lunch. It's strange to me.

Sometimes people are predisposed to see or to remain hard in heart. That's exactly what happened in John 12:27-30. The Father spoke audibly in response to a prayer that Jesus had just prayed. The Father said, *"I have both glorified it, and will glorify it again."* The people's response was interesting. Some said it thundered, others said an angel had spoken to Him. It's curious to me how some thought there was a natural explanation (thunder) and others recognized it was spiritual (angels spoke to Him), but not for them personally. Both interpretations were wrong. Jesus told them the voice came for their sake. The audible voice was for the people, not Jesus. He didn't need it to be audible. The Father made Himself known to the crowd by His voice, and yet they did not benefit from His efforts. Their unbelief (verse 12:37) became the filter that made them unable to hear what was spoken to them.

In the months that followed those early meetings at Bethel, I began to see things happen that I had hungered for, for as long as I could remember. I had always read about the God who healed and set free and had even seen it as a special moment in our church life. But I had never seen it on a large scale where it became the norm. This was such a moment.

ALL CREATION SPEAKS, EVEN DOGS

One of my life's experiences that has helped me in this regard centers around a German Shorthair Pointer that I had many years ago, named Rez. He was born and bred to hunt. It was in his blood. At times that drive seemed stronger than even his desire to eat. I had never seen anything like it. If he was released in a field, he would run patterns across the field, back and forth looking for a game bird that he would recognize by scent. Once he smelled the bird, he would lock into position, with his nose pointing to where the bird was hiding. That means if he was running in one direction, but the wind helped him to catch the scent of the bird in the opposite direction, he looked like a contortionist. His body was facing one way while his head/nose faced the opposite. Both his passion and skill were beautiful to behold.

He was also trained to hunt with another pointing dog. This pair of dogs is called a brace. One of the things they are taught is that if one dog is the first to smell the game bird and goes on point, the other dog goes on point immediately, even though they don't yet smell the bird. It's called *honoring the point.* Often when the second dog honors the point of the other dog, they eventually get to smell the same bird as the wind tends to shift. I've noticed the same in worship and other affectionate times with the Lord. Valuing the experience of another often opens the floodgates to an encounter of our own.

Valuing the experience of another often opens the floodgates to an encounter of our own.

It would be wisdom for all of us to recognize when another believer is being touched by God, and/or is in a place of deep recognition of His presence in worship. We get to shift our focus and *honor the point*— adjust our attitude, thoughts, and behavior as though we, too, were having a mighty encounter with God. It's not hypocrisy. Honoring the response of another believer is an act of faith, as we know God is no respecter of persons, and He's the same yesterday, today and forever. What He is doing for another person is as much our promise as it is for anyone. This is how faith works. Faith is anchored in the nature and promises of God.

I've had times when I've come into a service a bit ruffled by a well-meaning believer with inappropriate comments right before the meeting starts. To be honest, my attention is not on the Lord. I remember one time in particular getting settled in my front-row seat and looking down the row and seeing a dear friend who is a great lover of God with hands held high, exalting His name. I immediately threw my hands in the air as though I was in a deep place of affectionate expressions of praise to the Lord. It wasn't hypocrisy. I was honoring the point of another person's discovery. And it would be absolutely true to say, their encounter soon became my own. Every. Single. Time.

MAJOR TRANSITION

Prior to my coming, the church had grown to somewhere around 2800 people. By the time I arrived it was closer to 2000. I use these numbers only to illustrate something that is frequent in great moves of God.

When people think they know how God will come, they often leave disappointed, as He rarely "dances to our tune." He is God, the sovereign ruler over all. You can't invite the Lord of all to come and not expect Him to have His own ideas and plans that are often contrary to ours. What is perhaps the most shocking is that we derive our plans from what we see in Scripture. But then His plan will almost always include a part of Scripture we were unaware of or weren't particularly fond of. This is part of the test to see how hungry we really are. When we hunger for Him, casting aside any agendas we might have created, we are then much more prone to encounter Him, His way, and in His timing. My job is to hunger, and make it known. Leave the rest up to Him. He is good. His promise to us is to make Himself conspicuous. (See John 14:21.) He stated, *"Now suppose one of you fathers is asked by his son for a fish; he will not give him a snake instead of a fish, will he? . . . how much more will your heavenly Father give the Holy Spirit to those who ask Him?"* (Luke 11:11-13). The cry for revival is ultimately a cry for Him.

I am reminded of the parable Jesus gave about the man who bought a field. *"The kingdom of heaven is like a treasure hidden in the field, which a man found and hid again; and from joy over it he goes and sells all that he has and buys that field"* (Matt. 13:44). Revival is much like the treasure in the field. The field no doubt had parts that were not so attractive or valuable, but you had to buy it all to get the treasure.

We bought the field, and what a treasure we found. The treasure helped us to endure the unpleasant parts of the field that we now owned. On one hand, the presence of God was manifest in very pronounced ways, and His power was more commonly demonstrated with extraordinary miracles. And yet many left the church, and the critics came. My own denominational leaders told me that every single day they received calls of criticism about me.

Many pastors have found comfort in Gideon's story. His army was over 30,000 soldiers to start with but was reduced to 300 men before the battle began. I suppose all of us who have had people leave the church have found strength in Gideon's experience. And while sometimes I think it was the pastor's foolish behavior or poor communication that drove the sheep away, there's still comfort to be found. For me, the most amazing part of this story is that God didn't just reduce the size of the army so God could prove He could win with a few mismanaged soldiers. Instead, He reduced the army to the most courageous and alert solders Gideon had. The final number was insignificant. They simply had to share in the same character of courage and readiness for war. There were only 300 that fit that elite category. Of course, God could have won with 300 lazy, undisciplined cowards. Let's be honest, He doesn't need us at all. But He tends to work with surrendered human strength, skill, and ingenuity. He doesn't need what we have to offer. We are the ones in need. We have need to be used by Him. In part, our Christlike identity is developed through God using us for His purposes. And it is in that process we learn to refine our focus and commitment to excellence in all we are and do as an offering to Him.

DREAMS AND DEPARTURES

During this season in the move of God, He was very generous in giving me daily guidance. I don't want to suggest that He is ever not generous. But during this season He made His will unmistakable and nearly impossible for me to miss.

In the beginning of our journey, I had a dream about taking an off-ramp from a freeway and then going over the overpass so I could get on the same freeway, but go the opposite direction. In the dream, I could see that the off-ramp and overpass were very icy. This was a warning dream. I woke up knowing exactly what the Lord was saying. He was warning me to shift the direction of the church slowly in response to this new season so we wouldn't go off the road, causing unnecessary casualties. I shared it with our pastoral staff, and as best as I knew how, we took baby steps in entering this move of God as an organization. I kept every ministry going that I inherited and made no changes to schedules or plans. I explained and over explained what was happening in this outpouring, giving time for people to observe without any pressure to enter in. I taught from the Scriptures what moves of God look like and gave wonderful examples in history. We went slowly. But we still lost people. Lots of people. Somewhere around 1000 people left in the following months, which was about half of those who called Bethel home.

There's probably no way to say this without sounding brash, calloused or inconsiderate, but the departure of so many people had very little effect on Beni and me. We were able to go from two services on Sunday morning down to one. It was a refreshing season to be able to take extra time with the people, without the pressure of getting them off campus to do the next meeting. It wasn't that we didn't care about the people who were leaving. But in my list of *what is valuable to me*, church attendance was not there. It only hurts if it matters. And it didn't matter to me, as compared to the manifest presence of God. With Him came all the things I ached for in my heart in order to demonstrate the love and power of God: miracles, signs, and wonders. When He comes, His Kingdom is always within reach.

For what it's worth, Redding has an abundance of amazing churches. I know some of their pastors, and they too are hungry for a great move of God. We also know that not everyone belongs at Bethel, and we were comforted in knowing these people found other good churches to be a part of that would go at a pace or direction that was more suitable to them.

Interestingly, I had another dream about a year later. In this dream I was driving down a freeway lit up with sunlight but also wet from melted ice. I knew immediately that the ice had melted from the previous dream, and it was now full speed ahead! I told the staff that we no longer would have to be overly cautious about the speed of travel. We had permission to go all out in our pursuit of the more of God without the fear of causing unnecessary harm.

The departure of so many had little effect because what we had ached for over the years was now unfolding. The prayers of 25 years ago, from our youth group on these very streets, was now happening before my eyes. Miracles were becoming the norm.

I remember one eight-week stretch where seven people had cancer and/or their tumors disappear in our services. And then there was the woman in her 40s, who had never heard anything before, healed of deafness. With wonder she pointed to the speakers in the ceiling. I went to talk with her to have her tell me what exactly happened and soon realized she had no idea what I was saying. She had never heard sounds of any kind before. But she joyfully responded to our hand signals and sign language with joyful sounds, verifying she could hear. That week her family began to teach her to speak. Her first word was *Jesus*, which was a good place to start.

My goal has not been to grow a big church. I want to grow big people. So, the attendance issue mattered very little to us, except that as my dad always told us, "Each number represents a person." When what you value most happens, it makes up for all the unfortunate things that happen that weren't important enough to make it on your priority list. When you've ached for Jesus' name to be exalted through signs and wonders, the number of people in the room stops defining success or failure.

My goal has not been to grow a big church.
I want to grow big people.

I had one basic test that I took often at the end of the day with two questions: 1. Did God show up? 2. Did I do what He said? If I could say yes to those two things, it was a good day, regardless of the circumstances. It is also important for me to make something clear at this point: Yes, I did all I knew to do to honor the Lord and obey Him in taking risk and enduring difficulties because of how He showed up. And I honestly can't think of any direction or decision I would do differently. Having said that, I'm confident that my best still had flaws, and if I could see more clearly, I'd change some things. And I'm okay with that, as I am proof that He still works through imperfect people.

The painful part of the mass exodus was watching my pastoral staff lose many of their friends. Families were split. Parents stayed; young adult children left. And vice versa. Some of the leaders who brought us back to Bethel left. They brought us in with a 100% vote of support of the eldership. But many couldn't handle the mystery that comes in the outpouring. One of the families who left said, "We know this is God. We just can't do it." The amazing pastoral staff stayed true to me, and more importantly, to the measure of outpouring of the Spirit we were given. We were stewarding a gift from God. And that gift caused conflict. Any honest study of history will show this to be more common than any of us would like to admit.

SEEDS ATTRACT CONFLICT

As mentioned earlier in Chapter One, what God gives us in answer to our prayers is often the seed of what we asked for. There's an oak tree in the acorn. Faith sees the *oak tree in the acorn*. This helps us to live in the fear of God where it is needed most: stewarding well what He has put in our charge. Revival is most often given in that manner, in seed form.

A sobering lesson about the nature of the seeds that God plants in our lives is found in the Parable of the Seed and the Sower, Matthew 13:21. *"For when tribulation or persecution arises **because** of the Word . . .."* The Word of God is His seed, and that seed attracts conflict! And the way we navigate that conflict determines the measure of breakthrough we are able to enjoy. It's not a test of punishment. It is a test of mercy. If we are given more than we can bear, it will break us. But if we're given what we have the character to manage well, it will establish us.

Chapter Four

WHAT IS REVIVAL?

What we call revival is simply New Testament Christianity, the saints going back to normal.
—VANCE HAVNER

THE safety and integrity of any building is founded on the principle that the building itself must stay true to the foundation. The foundation of any building sets the parameters for what is to be built. And while there are times when the building itself will reach beyond the footprint set by the foundation, it is always held in place by that foundation. This is a simple yet critical point when we consider what the normal Christian life should look like. The Church was birthed in revival: the outpouring of the Holy Spirit with the overwhelming presence of God upon a people that changes us individually and corporately until it eventually impacts a city. This was our beginning, our foundation. Why should we expect to build upon anything less than God's heart revealed on that day? Everything built upon that foundation must live in honor of those same boundaries/values. But then, because that foundation can take greater weight, it must be built upon to take it to higher levels, as God always takes us from *glory to glory*.

THE NATURE OF REVELATION

God reveals things to us to increase our understanding of inheritance, as revealed truth draws us into a relationship with Him where our understanding illustrates the nature of His covenant with us. Revelation leads to experience, which in turn leads us to greater revelation. Truth stewarded well attracts greater truth. God always intended that stewarding truth well would take us to new levels of glory.

> The secret things belong to the Lord our God, but **the things revealed belong to us and to our sons forever,** that we may observe all the words of this law (Deuteronomy 29:29).

Revelation leads to experience, which in turn leads us to greater revelation. Truth stewarded well attracts greater truth.

This really is an astonishing statement. Whatever has been revealed in times past is our present possession. And that promise is eternal. This promise is God's perspective on what has been given to us, meaning it is settled in His mind. And yet if we look at history, we'd have to admit that some things were understood and practiced at previous times that are not as clear today. Any breakdown in the effectiveness of this promise is not on God's end of the equation. It's on ours. And the breakdown continues as long as we fall for the lie that our inferior demonstration of the power, purity, and love is what God ordained for this season. It's simply not true. He did not ordain lack. He stated that truth was to belong to us, and truth experienced always leads to freedom and liberty. These are the expressions of true citizens of His Kingdom. Somehow what they knew then was not kept at the forefront of their thinking or managed well in their lifestyle for the next generation to inherit. Truths are to be a part of our spiritual inheritance, revealing what God is calling us into.

> *"My Spirit which is upon you, and My words which I have put in your mouth shall not depart from your mouth, nor from the mouth of your offspring, nor from the mouth of your offspring's offspring," says the Lord, "from now and forever"* (Isaiah 59:21).

This promise overlaps the previous one from Deuteronomy 29:29, in that even the prophetic words were never to depart from our mouths, nor the mouths of our descendants, forever! God has always had a plan to incorporate the gifting and experiences of multiple generations into one ongoing expression of His purposes on earth. This is never clearer than in revival. Revival is truly where *Heaven invades earth.*

It probably needs to be stated here that when I talk about revelation, I'm not talking about adding to Scripture. The Bible is complete; don't add, don't take away. But we need revelation to understand what has already been written. When the Holy Spirit comes upon a person in revelation, it is a most wonderful experience. Sometimes it is extreme, usually with some sort of power encounter involved that expands our understanding of a subject or issue. And sometimes revelation comes in a very subtle way, which is usually primarily a cognitive level. Obviously extreme moments are easier to remember. But it is often the subtle that is where we are tested most, in that the prevailing question is this: Will we steward what was given until God has accomplished His purposes in us through that truth? These moments are primarily cognitive, in that they touch our mind/perception.

God has always had a plan to incorporate the gifting and experiences of multiple generations into one ongoing expression of His purposes on earth.

First of all, there is a level of truth that is common for all people with no need for additional revelation. As I understand it, there are three different witnesses that testify of our understanding of truth: 1. Creation itself speaks of the nature and existence of God. It reveals Him for all who are interested. 2. The laws of God are written on our hearts. You don't need to grow up in a civilized country to know that stealing is wrong. We carry that realization in our heart. 3. Jesus enlightens the heart and mind of every person who comes into the world. (See John 1:9.) It seems that this may be where *due north* is established in the heart, which is the absolute sense of right and wrong. Everyone receives that when they are born into this world. But there is more, and the Holy Spirit is needed for such increase. *"But when He, the Spirit of truth, comes, He will guide you into all the truth"* (John 16:13).

Every truth reveals the nature of God and is ultimately an invitation to enter into a relationship with Him in order to enter the promised lifestyle that illustrates the revelation given. Whenever God reveals truth to us, He is inviting us into ongoing experience that testifies of Him.

Mary, the mother of Jesus, illustrates this reality quite well.

I love the study of revival in Scripture and in Church history. The Old Testament story of Nineveh, addressed in the Book of Jonah, is mind-boggling, even for New Testament times. It might be one of the most underrated moments in all of history, certainly worthy of focused attention. And then there's the story of Ephesus in the New Testament, found in Acts 19. Each city saw an invasion of God's presence that brought transformation of life for their entire city.

Whenever God reveals truth to us, He is inviting us into ongoing experience that testifies of Him.

Each story in Scripture and in Church history provokes me to a pursuit of all that God has made available in my lifetime. But the problem I have with most studies on revival is that conclusions are made based on the history of revival, and not on the nature or promises of God. That means that when a revival ended due to greed, competition, self-promotion or the like, it is assumed that it was God's will for it to end. And while it is God who can bring an end to such an outpouring of the Holy Spirit, it was not because God no longer wanted a revival. It was because He refused to align His outpouring with the soulish attempts of His people to control and direct Him. Perhaps the best illustration for this is the biblical responsibility of priests of the Old Testament, with the fire on the altar. It was God who lit the fire on the altar, but it was the priests who kept it burning. It is the same today. God initiates the mighty outpouring of His Spirit (fire), and we sustain or correctly steward the outpouring for His glory and the transformation of cities and nations, which is still in His heart.

And the fire on the altar shall be kept burning on it; it shall not be put out. And the priest shall burn wood on it every morning, and lay the burnt offering in order on it; and he shall burn on it the fat of the peace offerings. A fire shall always be burning on the altar; it shall never go out (Leviticus 6:12-13 NKJV).

For a simpler example, consider this: Since revivals rarely last past two years, the common thought is that revivals are to be the occasional visitation of God to give a boost to an otherwise failing or weak Church. It rarely takes into account that God lifted the anointing for revival because of the sins or compromises of those leading it, which none of us would support.

God will often bless the unbeliever before He blesses the carnality of the Church. The blessing of God upon the unbeliever is His invitation, or calling card, for them to come and taste more of His goodness. As it is written, it's His *"kindness that leads us to repentance"* (see Rom. 2:4). Blessing upon the unrighteous calls them to the source of that blessing, the Father. But if He blesses the carnality of the Church, He strengthens our independence, rebellion, need to be in charge. Throughout history He lifts His favor and blessings from the group of people who have entered into self-promotion, jealousy, and building personal empires from the move of God. Revivals have more than their share of such careless responses to the favor of God given in times of outpouring. He lifts the glory from us for our protection.

PENTECOST, THE TRUE FOUNDATION

The Scripture says that the apostle and prophet are the foundation of the Church. (See Ephesians 2:20.) But Pentecost is the foundation of church life, in that it was their introduction to the filling and empowerment of the Holy Spirit. That made everything that was thought to be impossible for the child of God now quite doable. This was most likely the greatest paradigm shift in all of history. Now, frail humanity had access to the divine in which, through grace, they were enabled to do what only the Son of God could do. That in essence is what grace is: divine favor given through the enabling presence of God. This was sure to change everything for all who see it as it really is.

It could be said that if there was ever a meeting that people didn't control, defile, or redirect according to their opinions or religious preferences, it would have to be the gathering of 120 persons on the day of Pentecost. (See Acts 2:1-21.) No one knew enough to get it wrong. Those involved in this life-changing event first invaded Heaven with their prayers and intercessions for ten days. And yet they had no clue what God was about to do. They just knew they were to pray and then He would do something new. As a result, they became the target of Heaven. And Heaven hit its mark by taking a small crowd of hungry and humble people and changing the known world through them. Should it not be of concern to us that we have not continued with the nature and Spirit of our beginnings? Obviously, I believe it should be a primary concern. We can't guilt or shame our way back to the foundation. But we can repent, confess, and earnestly pray our way back.

When Jesus addressed the issue of first love that was missing in the Church at Ephesus in Revelation 2:4, He told them to return to the deeds they did in the beginning. Perhaps that would be good advice for us as well. Again, we see the biblical emphasis on sustaining *what got us here*—our foundation. Our beginnings must be recognized, honored, and valued for them to be of use in all that we're building. We must not forget what got us here. It wasn't technology, brilliant programs with lighting and sound. Neither was it through great campaigns and united endeavors by multiple churches involved, as valuable as these things are. It was Him. He became pronounced and conspicuous in and upon the Church through the outworking of the Holy Spirit, in and through His people. Yielded people, sometimes ignorant and simple, are the greatest tools in the hand of the Lord.

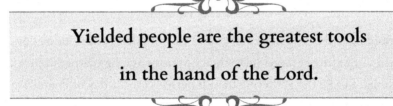

Yielded people are the greatest tools in the hand of the Lord.

LEARNING FROM CULTURE

One of my all-time favorite commercials is a United Airlines commercial from 1990. I bring it up on YouTube every once in a while, to watch again. I've even played it for our staff. In the commercial the owner of a business announces, "I got a phone call this morning from one of our oldest customers. He fired us. After 20 years, he fired us. He said he didn't know us anymore. I think I know why. We used to do business with a handshake. Face to face. Now it's a phone call. Then a fax. 'I'll get back to you later.' With another fax, probably. Well folks, something's got to change. That's why we're going to set out with our little face-to-face chat with every customer we have." One of the guys objects saying, "But Ben, that's got to be over 200 cities!" To which the boss responds, "I don't care." At this point someone comes in with a stack of airline tickets. He then hands them out to each of his team members. Then one of the guys asks the owner where he was going. He answers, "To visit that old friend who fired us this morning."

I have to admit tears come to my eyes at the most embarrassing times, not always when it would seem reasonable to others in the room. And this is one of those times. It moves me in ways that are hard to explain. It is so easy in ministry to forget what got us to the place where we are tasting some measure of the blessing and favor of God. Our problem is that we supposedly become experts, leaving behind the simplicity of childlike faith and obedience that brought us to that place of breakthrough. It is the honest and authentic, face-to-face connection with God and His people that He values. This example, silly as it may seem to some, illustrates what is important in church life in general and is critical in revival. We must maintain the simplicity of devotion to Christ that brought us into a place of significant outpouring. That role of continually placing ourselves on the altar of His mighty work is what keeps the fire burning.

ORIGINAL DESIGN

Many years ago, I heard a great leader in the Body of Christ recount a fun story he experienced as a pastor. The congregation was growing wonderfully and had run out of room. In response, they were building a new sanctuary. Personally, he had no building skills, whatsoever, but wanted to be involved somehow. Finally, the contractor found something he could trust the pastor to be able to do. (I don't remember the actual numbers for this story, but the principle is untouched.)

He asked the pastor if he could cut 100 two-by-fours to a length of eight feet. The pastor was excited to be involved. So, after everyone left for the day, he began to work on his assignment. He took the first board, measured eight feet in length with his tape measure, marked it with his pencil and cut the board. He then put the tape measure away and used the newly cut board to measure his next one. He figured it would be a lot easier than having to use the tape measure 99 more times. He drew a line at the end of the board. He then removed the previously cut board, put it in a stack and cut the one with the fresh pencil line. He then took that newly cut board, placed it on top of the next one and cut it. The problem with that method of measurement is that each time he measured from the previously cut board and drew a line, it was about one eighth of an inch too long. That wouldn't be much of a problem if he was only cutting two or three boards. But having each of the 100 boards about an eighth of an inch longer than the previous put the boards at the end of the job around nine feet in length. His assignment was to cut them to eight feet. Small deviations amount to great errors over time.

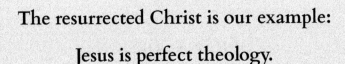

The resurrected Christ is our example:

Jesus is perfect theology.

This is a powerful lesson for me personally, as it speaks about adhering to the original standard for what God intends to do in our lifetime. The resurrected Christ is our example: Jesus is perfect theology. We often approach church life this way, comparing ourselves with the previous generation with only *an eighth-inch difference*. But after 2000 years of eighth-inch differences, we have a Church with values, priorities, and lifestyles that don't look anything like the original standard found in Jesus Christ. And to top it off, many consider it a virtue not to pursue deliverance, healing, salvation and cultural transformation. Jesus described His intent this way:

> *Truly, truly, I say to you, he who believes in Me, the works that I do, he will do also; and greater works than these he will do; because I go to the Father. Whatever you ask in My name, that will I do, so that the Father may be glorified in the Son. If you ask Me anything in My name, I will do it. If you love Me, you will keep My commandments* (John 14:12–15).

That passage, backed by our Master's personal lifestyle of love, miracles, and purity, is the eight-foot-long board. What we have in most of our churches is the board that keeps getting cut an eighth of an inch longer than the previous generation and/or movement until 2000 years later, we end up with church life that bears little resemblance to the standard. To make matters worse, we leaders redefine what we're supposed to be doing to fit what we're good at. That way, we can feel good about ourselves and our success. I'm not in this to feel good about myself. I'm in this because He called me to Himself and gave me life. And now I am responsible to do what He said, believe what He promised, and obey His commission, all in the context of love and purity.

When I say these kinds of things, it is never to bring shame or guilt. That doesn't help. In fact, my desire is quite the opposite. Making such decrees is to give each one an invitation to true Kingdom-like hunger. It's an invitation to pursue and embrace all that God has promised and purposed for our lives and ultimately for this generation. We just can't get away with reducing our assignment to what we're good at. For example, I may never be good at a miracle lifestyle. It makes no difference. We are called into this and must take it seriously. And in response to the call, I must embrace it with my whole heart.

JESUS, THE PERSON OF REVIVAL

Jesus is revival personified. So many things stand out in examining the life of Christ, each of which testifies to the life of revival: His compassion, wisdom, powerful teaching and insights, miracles, and His ability to draw those who seemed to be the least deserving to Him. Volumes have been written just describing His life and His impact. Revival is rediscovering the beauty and wonder of Jesus. He, through the working of the Holy Spirit, comes to the forefront of our thinking once again in every great move of God. For me it is His power, His love, His wisdom, and His purity. Those four things express to me who Jesus is. And they express the nature of revival. As Leonard Ravenhill puts it, "God is one pent-up revival."[1]

I believe it is natural for us to be drawn to different aspects of His life. We find ourselves attracted to what has impacted us the most. The way He treated the woman caught in adultery illustrates His compassion beautifully and is an expression of revival. His love for children, unwilling for the disciples to make it all about the grown-ups, stands out to others. The point is, we are all attracted to different things about Jesus. And while I am especially moved by specific stories, I don't have the luxury of deciding what parts of His life I am willing to follow.

Jesus is revival personified.

I've heard people react to an emphasis on healing by saying, "Healing is not the whole Gospel." And my response is, "Yes, that's true. But neither is it whole without it." It's a part of a much bigger message: Salvation is to touch the whole man—spirit, soul, and body. But sometimes when something is ignored, or set aside because it causes controversy or pain, then it's time to emphasize it for a season until it's healthy enough to be sustained as a normal part of our lifestyle. But until then, it receives extra emphasis to bring it into its rightful place. We do that with our diets. Sometimes we're lacking in certain things, so we boost our intake of vitamin C, for example, until our health becomes more stable.

Often when things are emphasized by a certain group or person, another person will say, "That teaching is out of balance." I remember when I first heard someone teach on balance; it was a liberating word, because it carried with it the understanding that we often need to embrace conflicting ideas or practices to come into a place of health. But to be honest, most of the time I hear the word used today, it's to tell me what I can't have. It's prohibitive, not inviting. For many, balance is middle of the road, somewhere in between joy and depression, or between hot and cold. That's not the Gospel. But if *balance* to you means "red-hot for the power of the Holy Spirit," and "red-hot in your passion for the Word of God," then call me balanced. That is my pursuit. It's never to be either/or.

HE BECOMES CONSPICUOUS

Revival is a season where God's presence becomes manifested much more openly. His presence and His will become what the hungry are pre-occupied with. In revival, it is the nearness of God that becomes the most dominating factor. Some would argue that God is with us always, and that revivals are mere hype over what already exists. It is true that He is with us and will never leave us. But as true as that statement is, it is equally incomplete in every way. He makes Himself conspicuous to those who hunger for Him, as it was He who promised, *"I will be found by you"* (Jer. 29:14).

I've seen times when the presence of God is so pronounced in a gathering that musicians couldn't play, singers couldn't sing, preachers couldn't preach, and the need for Christian activities all but vanished. Why? He is among us, and nothing else matters. The awareness of His presence is so pronounced that everything else fades into obscurity. Schedules dissolve, anxieties disappear, and reconciliation is in the air. The need to do something to satisfy our definition of a good meeting goes away while confession, repentance, and restoration in relationships become common, although they are seldom the direction given from the platform. In such moments I've had people ask me to invite people to faith in Christ. "When are you going to give an altar call?" Others have been miraculously healed when no one is praying for healing. And still others obtain the sound mind that was promised to them in their salvation. The mightier the manifest presence of God is among us, the less there is for us to do, except, of course, respond to Him. He leads in the dance, and ours is to follow. Our role in directing the meeting ceases. He is here. And He is Lord.

The beauty of this kind of gathering, *that we cannot conjure up*, is that the glory experienced in the corporate meeting often follows us home. Peace and joy fill our homes in new ways, while our workplace goes through a transformation of its own. Sometimes people want to know what is different about us. They can sense something has happened, but can't put their finger on it. There are other times that His presence is upon me in such a strong way that I can't sleep. Sometimes it's the fire of His presence, sometimes it's His raw power. I don't analyze it. But neither will I ask Him to remove it. I assume it is His way of summoning me to Himself, and I must say yes.

I suppose it also needs to be said that in such times of glorious presence, He equally leads us into the disciplined study of the Word, into small groups for meaningful relationships, and wonderful times of thanksgiving, praise and worship. He's the one who leads us into the most meaningful parts of life, each in their own place and in their own time. We can and must always trust His lead.

There are many ways to describe this mysterious but wonderful grace that is released over the people of God. We usually define it by what we value most in the Gospel, whether it be souls saved, bodies healed, or a new grace for worship and the priority in the gathering to delight in His presence. All of this, and more, is true. But it's best to leave the direction up to Him and learn to follow His lead.

ACTS CHAPTER TWO

Many would agree that the Church was born on the day of Pentecost in Acts 2. This whole chapter is revival. I personally believe that at least 11 of them were already born again, as Jesus released the Holy Spirit to them in John 20. This happened before Pentecost.

And when He had said this, He breathed on them and said to them, "Receive the Holy Spirit" (John 20:22).

Since every believer receives the Holy Spirit when they are born again, it seems to me that this was the moment when the eleven remaining disciples were converted. So, when they were instructed to stay in Jerusalem for the *"promise of the Father,"* to be clothed with the *"power from on high,"* and *"baptized in the Holy Spirit"* (see Acts 1:4; Luke 24:49; and Acts 1:5, respectively)—different wording for the same experience—it was to help them to obtain what they didn't get in their conversion.

In order for these disciples to function as Jesus had planned, they would need both power and authority. The disciples were given authority in their commission, in Matthew 28:19. But they also needed power, which could come only through an encounter. I know many will differ with me on this point of the baptism in the Spirit being a *second touch*, which is fine. Just don't miss that fact that power comes in the encounter. Being *"clothed with power from on high"* was never meant to be reduced to a doctrine or a point in our statement of faith. It was an experience. An encounter. It was the beginning of a relational journey that would introduce His followers to a lifestyle of superior reasoning in every possible way. It was the kind of reasoning that had as its anchor, *"nothing is impossible with God"* (see Luke 1:37). And having that as a foundation changes everything.

Our encounter in the baptism in the Holy Spirit is the outpouring that forever changed the course of human history. Now, instead of Jesus, the anointed Son of God walking the earth, demonstrating the wonder of God's Kingdom through revealing the Father's heart, potentially millions of His followers can be clothed with the same power. It is all made possible because of this day called Pentecost. It is a beautiful gift of God's grace. But the errors of some have caused many to back away from this kind of lifestyle, convinced that it is too dangerous to try. To my way of thinking, it is too dangerous not to. After all, His will reigns over all of our wills— *"on earth as it is in Heaven."*

A BRIDE IS BORN

In a very real sense the birth of the Church, which is the Bride of Christ, was made possible with the prophetic act of a spear piercing the side of Jesus. As Eve was taken from Adam's side, when the Father took a rib and fashioned woman, even so the Bride of Christ was taken from Jesus' side when He was pierced with the spear. The basis for the Church's existence came forth when blood and water poured forth. Of this the prophet spoke: *"In that day a fountain will be opened for the house of David and for the inhabitants of Jerusalem, **for sin and for impurity"*** (Zech. 13:1). Blood deals with sin and water, as in, *"the washing of the water with the word of God"* (see Eph. 5:26), deals with impurity and the contamination of living in a sinful world. Those two expressions of grace from God make the Church, His spotless Bride, possible.

The Old Testament priests had a similar practice we can learn from. When they entered the tabernacle grounds, they first encountered the brazen altar upon which animal sacrifices, with the shedding of blood, were made to postpone the penalty of sin for one more year. But following the need for blood to be shed, they still needed the washing of water. This was done at the next station called the laver. It was here that they dealt with the contamination that comes from their ministry assignments. It wasn't about their sins. That was dealt with in the shedding of blood at the brazen altar. It was because they lived in an impure environment. If ever there was a lesson for us regarding the need for the continual input and cleansing of the Word of God, it is here. It cleanses. And at the same time, like a sword it cuts deep, mysteriously bringing healing to where it cuts.

In essence, revival is made possible by encountering God. That encounter, regardless how extreme or how subtle, carries with it the seed of revival, which is the seed of reformation—that which could change a nation if stewarded well. Look at it this way: There's an oak tree in an acorn if the acorn is taken care of properly. But there is also a forest of oak trees available through the seeds of the one oak tree. The outcome is written into the nature of the seed, but it requires proper stewardship by the caregivers, in this case, those affected by the revival. So it is with one touch from God. It carries the seed of transformation, not only for our lives, but is enough for a nation. This is the responsibility that comes with encountering God.

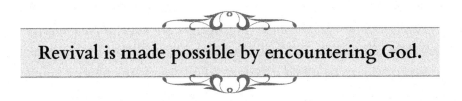

Revival is made possible by encountering God.

CHARACTERISTICS OF REVIVAL

1. They occurred in times of moral darkness and national depression;

2. Each began in the heart of a consecrated servant of God who became the energizing power behind it;

3. Each revival rested on the Word of God, and most were the result of proclaiming God's Word with power;

4. All resulted in a return to the worship of God;

5. Each witnessed the destruction of idols where they existed;

6. In each revival, there was a recorded separation from sin;

7. In every revival the people returned to obeying God's laws;

8. There was a restoration of great joy and gladness;

9. Each revival was followed by a period of national prosperity.[2]

SO, WHO WAS OFFENDED?

I found it interesting that many of the manifestations that we were told would offend the unbeliever only offended the believer unwilling to change. I was somewhat surprised that most unbelievers hardly took note of what makes many Christians angry. They seemed to expect the supernatural (things they couldn't understand) to be present if God is there. People expect it to drive unbelievers away. For the most part, the outpouring only drove believers away who were taught that anything outside of their regular church attendance and personal disciplines was not from God. If we could learn anything from the outpouring of the Spirit in Acts 2, it's that even among those who mocked and were confused, there were 3000 souls added to the Church in one day. If we want the same fruit and breakthrough seen in the early Church, we'll have to take our hands off the reins of what God is directing.

If we want the same fruit and breakthrough seen in the early Church, we'll have to take our hands off the reins of what God is directing.

NOTES

1. Leonard Ravenhill, *Why Revival Tarries*, (Bloomington, MN: Bethany House Publishers, 2004), 140.

2. Winkie Pratney, *Revival: Principles to Change the World,* (Christian Life Books, 2002), 13.

Chapter Five

PRAYING FOR REVIVAL

Every outpouring of the Spirit is preceded by earnest,
agonizing, intercession, accompanied by a heart-
brokenness and humiliation before God.
—LEONARD RAVENHILL[1]

PRAYER is, without question, the number-one ingredient or tool used to bring about revival. In book after book on the history of revival, this feature is highlighted as the premier issue. I believe this to be absolutely true. A wonderful verse in this regard is, *"Ask rain from the Lord at the time of the spring rain"* (Zech. 10:1). Prophetically speaking, this rain is the outpouring of the Holy Spirit also addressed in Joel 2. I do find it interesting that we are commanded to pray for something that is either already happening or is supposed to happen in the season we are in—*day of latter rain.* Praying in this manner properly aligns us with God's heart, which is a core value of prayer.

But I must admit that I have difficulty with this as well, as I've read of countless great leaders in the Body of Christ who have prayed for revival, some for decades, but died without ever experiencing one. Many wonderful men of God in England, for example, prayed for a move of God, and even visited the outpouring that was happening in Wales, and yet never experienced it for themselves. I don't want to criticize any of them, as they have rightfully gone down in history as leaders who truly lived for Jesus and impacted nations through their holy lifestyles and powerful ministries. Yet I don't believe it was the will of God for these men and women to miss out on what they were praying for.

> Prayer is, without question, the number-one ingredient or tool used to bring about revival.

CHARLES FINNEY SETS A STANDARD

Charles Finney was one of America's greatest revivalists. His personal journey seems to set a pattern for entering into the greater things of God, especially as it pertains to prayer followed by breakthrough. I want us to walk together through a small part of his story to help see the testimony of this world changer, understanding that the same God of Charles Finney lives in us.[2] We can and must expect more.

Finney wrote about his first encounters with prayer meetings and their apparent lack of answers to their prayers. This was in his pre-conversion state. Those attending the prayer meetings once asked him if he'd like for them to pray for him. He told them no. He said it was because he didn't see God answering their prayers. He confessed he probably needed prayer, as he was aware of his sinfulness. But it didn't appear that it would do any good for them to pray for him, as they were continually asking things of God, but they never seemed to receive. In fact, they had been praying for years for a revival, but still complained of their leanness of soul. He said, "You have prayed enough since I have attended these meetings to have prayed the devil out of [their city]. But here you are, praying on and complaining still."[3] He later acknowledged that he realized that these were genuine and sincere people who were true followers of Christ. But no one had ever taught them how to pray and get results.

Finney stated, "This inconsistency, the fact that they prayed so much and were not answered, was a sad stumbling block to me."[4] Please take note, one of the great witnesses to our being people of faith is that we have answers to prayers. In fact, I like to challenge our people with this charge: You owe God answers to your prayers, and you owe people answers to your prayers. I know it sounds like a wrong statement to make. But consider this. We tend to think statements like that are wrong because we think our unanswered prayers are God's fault, which we call "God's sovereignty." I say it isn't. We must come to the realization that the lack of answers to prayers is not on God's end of the equation. It is on ours. God's covenant and promise are more than adequate for us to have a lifestyle filled with answered prayers. The adjustment is up to us.

FINNEY'S BAPTISM OF FIRE

Finney would later experience a dramatic conversion and baptism in the Spirit that positioned him to impact a nation with the Gospel. He describes that experience:

> I must have continued in this state for a good while.... I returned to the front office, and found that the fire that I had made of large wood was nearly burned out. But as I turned and was about to take a seat by the fire, I received a

mighty baptism of the Holy Ghost. Without any expectation of it, without ever having the thought in my mind that there was any such thing for me, without any recollection that I had ever heard the thing mentioned by any person in the world, the Holy Spirit descended upon me in a manner that seemed to go through me, body and soul. I could feel the impression, like a wave of electricity, going through and through me. Indeed it seemed to come in waves and waves of liquid love; for I could not express it in any other way. It seemed like the very breath of God. I can recollect distinctly that it seemed to fan me, like immense wings.

No words can express the wonderful love that was shed abroad in my heart. I wept aloud with joy and love; and I do not know but I should say, I literally bellowed out unutterable gushings of my heart. These waves came over me, and over me, and over me, one after the other, until I recollect I cried out, "I shall die if these waves continue to pass over me." I said, "Lord, I cannot bear any more"; yet I had no fear of death.[5]

Throughout history, people have had life-changing encounters with God. Again, some of them are power-centered and some cognitive. But each injects the life of the believer with a grace to bring about transformation to the world around them. Finney became such a carrier of the presence of God that he became known as one who could affect his surroundings without ever saying a word.

The presence of God upon this man was so strong that he once walked into a factory and stood before the workers, but said nothing. One by one they fell to their knees, confessing their sins, turning their hearts to Jesus. Here is the story in his words:

I approached slowly, looking on each side at the machinery, as I passed; but observed that this girl grew more and more agitated, and could not proceed with her work. When I came within eight or ten feet of her, I looked solemnly at her. She observed it, and was quite overcome, and sunk down, and burst into tears. The impression caught almost like powder, and in a few moments nearly all in the room were in tears. This feeling spread through the factory. Mr. W__, the owner of the establishment, was present, and seeing the state of things, he said to the superintendent, "Stop the mill, and let the people attend to religion; for it is more important that our souls should be saved than that this factory run." The gate was immediately shut down, and the factory stopped; but where should we assemble? The superintendent suggested that the mule room was large; and, the mules being run up, we could assemble there. We did so, and a more powerful meeting I scarcely ever attended. It went on with great power. The building was large, and had many people in it, from the garret to the cellar. The revival went through the mill with astonishing power, and in the course of a few days nearly all in the mill were hopefully converted.[6]

This is truly one of my favorite stories in revival history. It underlines the absolute dependence upon the presence of the Holy Spirit upon us to accomplish His purposes while illustrating the critical factor of pointing people to Jesus in repentance. It is truly beautiful as it underscores that the purpose of prayer is to be possessed by God.

There are a great number of stories of how God supernaturally used this one man. Many of them are hard to believe as we have become accustomed to lack.

His stories are spectacular. And while Finney is a household name among students of revival, not everyone knows the name of Daniel Nash. This great man of prayer would go ahead of Finney to the towns he was about to visit. He went there to pray. Period. The impact of his prayers was so great that the revival they would soon experience would convert the whole town. The impact of the revival and the corresponding conversions brought about cultural changes and improvements to society in general. As has happened throughout revival history, crime would stop, alcoholism ended, and the police had little to do. In some places, even the jails were empty for years following the Finney revival. Interestingly, Finney stopped traveling and doing revival meetings after Nash went to be with the Lord. Why? He knew. The strength and breakthroughs of his ministry were brought on by the intercessions of this mostly unknown man—unknown here, but well known and celebrated in Heaven.

ARGENTINA—OMAR CABRERA PRAYS

I had the privilege of meeting Omar Cabrera in the late '90s while traveling to Argentina with Randy Clark. He was one of the great revivalists there, who also knew how to pray and get results. Some of the miracles of his meetings still stand out in my mind today as some of the greatest acts of God in Church history. It was such a joy to hear from this giant in the faith. Miracles filled his life, and he planted churches all across the great nation of Argentina through the revival he carried.

Randy often talks about the times he spent with Omar, as well as when he spoke in the churches he planted. They didn't have to be convinced of God's goodness or His power. These churches were started through the miracle invasion of God into their impossible situations through Omar's ministry. And as glorious as those stories are, I am most deeply moved by his stories of how he prayed.

Omar explained how he would go to a given city, get a hotel room, and pray. Sometimes he prayed for thirty days before starting his revival-type meetings. It's not a formula. He didn't pray to fill his quota. He prayed until he sensed a breakthrough in the Spirit. We often don't pray until there's breakthrough because we haven't yet learned to recognize the presence of God in ways that He has made available to us. Once Omar sensed the breakthrough in the Spirit, he would start the meetings. It's important to understand that these meetings didn't necessarily start with large crowds even though Omar had felt the breakthrough anointing. But such a strong miracle breakthrough would take place with the small crowd that great numbers of people would soon flock to the meetings. These meetings ignited the spirit of revival in city after city, with the ongoing testimony of the miracle works of God flourishing in those cities.

PRAYING INTO BREAKTHROUGH

My brother Bob is ten years younger than me. When he was 11 months old, he almost died. In fact, the doctors said he came within hours of death. My grandparents, my mom's parents, had a little boy die when he was 11 months old. Needless to say, they were deeply moved by my brother's condition and our family's situation. I'll never forget how my grandfather knelt in the living room to pray. He started in the morning and was there for hours. He got up around 2 in the afternoon, and said to the family, "Bobby will be fine." When my parents arrived back at the hospital, the doctors greeted them with the good news. "Something happened today around 2 o'clock, and Bobby will be fine." Praying until there's a breakthrough is the secret. But learning to recognize the breakthrough is the challenge.

How can we grow in our ability to recognize the breakthrough in the Spirit before it is worked out in our circumstances? It's completely through recognizing His presence. The four methods God uses most often to train us in this area are prayer (two-way conversation), the reading of Scripture (where we recognize Him highlighting a passage or phrase), listening to the preaching of the Word (where we learn to sense a shift in the atmosphere through the word spoken), and worship.

Revivals are never the result of token prayers.

If the prayers don't move me,

they won't move Him.

We often pray enough to ease our conscience, but not enough to make a difference. Revivals are never the result of token prayers. If the prayers don't move me, they won't move Him. How do you know when you've prayed into a breakthrough? By doing it, over and over again. It's in the process, with Him, that we learn to recognize His heart in a given situation. His presence changes in the ebb and flow of our prayers. It's possible to learn to recognize Him in the same way we can recognize whether our dearest friend is happy or sad, concerned or at ease. We are on a relational journey with God. We can learn to recognize His heart.

It's vital that we learn how to recognize the spirit of breakthrough. This happens first because we've learned to carry the burden of the Lord in prayer. When that burden lifts, we know it is finished or at least something has changed. Sometimes you can see breakthrough because your requests turn into decrees. Sometimes it's because you are unusually thankful for the answer before you see it manifest fully. Giving thanks always is a huge part of our life of faith. But I'm not talking here about thanksgiving as a calculated, disciplined response to Him to show you trust Him. I'm referring to the fact that unfathomable joy has sprung up in our hearts, and there is no other explanation, except the prayer has been answered. In the place of a burden, there is joy. In the place of cries of intercession, there are decrees of God's great promises and assured victories. All of us can learn these various ways of recognizing when the spirit of breakthrough is upon us. And it is at this time we must act!

THE ACT OF FAITH

Faith comes from the heart, not the mind. And yet faith is demonstrated through actions, for *"faith without works is dead"* (see James 2:17). Here is the reason I wanted to write this chapter and have been working to prepare you for this simple, but critical, yet often overlooked, point. Prayers of faith must be followed by an action of faith. Prayers for revival require action consistent with the nature of the prayers we've prayed.

Prayers of faith must be followed by an action of faith.

I'll never forget the wonderful privilege of hearing Dr. Paul Yonggi Cho speak when I was a young man. He is the pastor of the Full Gospel Church of Seoul, Korea, which is often referred to as the world's largest church. It has close to one million members. I have since had the honor of meeting him and spending time with him in his office with my dear friend Che Ahn. What a glorious time we had. Especially when he prayed for us. Wow!

Asked what was the key to the incredible breakthroughs he had seen in his lifetime, he answered, "I pray, and I obey." That was it. It's almost too simple. Perhaps that's the reason many have heard his secret and few have followed it completely. We are much like the leprous general who was told to dip himself in the river seven times to be healed. He refused because it was humiliating. It was too simple to meet his great need. His servant then reminded him that if he was asked to do something great and noble, he would do it. Why not also do it when the command is so simple? He followed the direction given and was healed. Here it is again, uncomplicated: pray and obey.

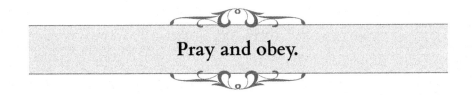

Pray and obey.

THE OLD TESTAMENT SPEAKS

There's a story in the Book of Joshua that God has used to illustrate this profound lesson given by Dr. Cho. The *pray-and-obey* assignment has a specific application that must be embraced for us to see continual breakthrough in our lives. Let's take a look at the story of Jericho to find what we need at this point. The story is found in Joshua 6:6-16. I'll summarize but encourage you to study this on your own.

The children of Israel were to march around the city of Jericho in absolute silence for six days. The Ark of the Covenant was with them. On the seventh day, they were to march around the city seven times. That was also done in silence. At the end of that Joshua commanded them, "Shout, for the Lord has given you the city!" And they did. The walls of that city fell flat.

> *So the people shouted, and priests blew the trumpets; and when the people heard the sound of the trumpet, the people shouted with a great shout and the wall fell down flat, so that the people went up into the city, every man straight ahead, and they took the city.*
>
> *They utterly destroyed everything in the city, both man and woman, young and old, and ox and sheep and donkey, with the edge of the sword* (Joshua 6:20-21).

This process of marching around the city is a type of our journey of prayer. They marched (prayed) as they were supposed to. And at the right moment there was an undeniable expression of faith for the victory at hand. The shout! Then the walls fell. But what seems to be a lost art in the Church is that we often have the prayer meetings, and even the shout, but forget that we have to go into the realm we've prayed to possess through the use of our power and authority. Israel still had to go into the city and defeat it. The point is, our *prayers remove the obstacles to victory,* but *it's the act of faith that takes us into the city to take possession of what we've obtained in prayer.* The Scripture, *"now the kingdom of heaven suffers violence, and violent men take it by force"* (Matt. 11:12), comes to mind at this point. Faith, and its corresponding actions, are the demonstrations of violence in the spirit realm. Evan Roberts knew this well when he said, "Power ridicules the strength of the enemy."

THE LIFE OF MIRACLES

I'm often asked about how to increase the miracle realm in a believer's life. I don't have a 1, 2, 3-step process. But what I have learned is patterned after the story of Jericho. I pray. I get alone with God, where I make my requests known. Prayer is like marching around a city. Sometimes these are extended times of prayer and sometimes brief. But they must be genuine, in that they move me deeply to a place of radical pursuit of, and surrender to, His will. I know breakthrough is imminent when I sense my prayers turning into decrees.

Prayers of this nature must be followed by acts of faith. It helped me so much to hear John Wimber spell faith, R. I. S. K. That was the simple change I needed in my pursuit of the miracles that validate the Gospel. *Risk* means I must now look for problems that only God could solve. It may be cancer, it may be drug addiction, or any one of a million other issues the enemy has brought into people's lives. Regardless of the problem, Jesus is willing and able to solve it.

We must make room for God to act if we're going to see this happen on a continual basis. If it's a meeting, create time to pray for the sick. If it's your home or business, stay tuned to those you encounter that have needs. The point is, He is the extravagant one. It's vital that we make room for Him to come and do what only He can do.

When the cancer disappears, the deaf ears are opened, or the torment of addiction leaves, we celebrate and give thanks to God. There must be expressions of joy. It's unnatural not to have joy when God is working. Throughout the Bible, praise responses to God burst forth when a miracle happens. We must take none of the glory for ourselves but give Him ALL the glory for the wonderful thing He has just done. But when the cancer doesn't leave or the addiction remains, I must go back to the prayer closet and pray some more. As simple as it may sound, my life is one of celebration, giving thanks and praise for answers, and also returning to the place of prayer because of the lack of a breakthrough. Back and forth, back and forth. Pray and obey. It is simple, yet profound.

REVIVAL PRAYING

Most everything I've described in this chapter is related to personal breakthroughs and victories. This is not an accident. Great moves of God usually start with one person. And that one person stewards what God has given them until that fire spreads, impacting large numbers of people and regions, and/or movements are changed.

We had horrific fires here in Redding a few years ago. There was a point where it looked like almost the entire city would go up in flames. Massive fires actually create their own weather system, which happened in our case. It was a disaster unlike anything we had ever experienced before. Thankfully, the wind shifted. And while well over 200,000 acres burned, including nearly 1100 homes, plus businesses, it was poised to do more.

If it's possible to picture this kind of extreme, out-of-control fire and turn it into something positive, then you get the picture of revival praying. Revival and revival praying create their own weather system. This is where everything else in our lives is brought into this singular focus and purpose—the move of God. Many want a revival, if it can fit nicely in their schedule. And while there are aspects of life that must continue, they become radically defined by this visitation of God that is marking everyone it touches with eternal purpose. Perhaps it can be said that our contentment in absence of revival is the actual hindrance to revival.

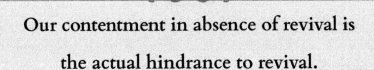

Our contentment in absence of revival is the actual hindrance to revival.

REBUILDING THE ALTAR

The restoration of the spiritual life of Israel often started with rebuilding the altar. Revivals begin in the same way. The altar was the place where sacrifices were made and deep repentance was demonstrated. The stones of the altar were uncut stones, meaning that coming before God in surrender was never to be shaped by our design or control of the moment. Coming to God has always been through grace. Our dreams, ambitions, sins, and successes must be laid on the altar of surrender. Do our dreams matter? Yes and no. They are of great importance in their rightful place, as they reveal the nature, promises, and covenant of God. But out of place, they are destructive in that they compete for the affections and devotion that are only to be given to God. The words of Jesus speak to this reality: *"Seek first the Kingdom of God, and His righteousness, and all these things will be added unto you"* (Matt. 6:33). When the Kingdom of God is first in our pursuit, we can be trusted with fulfilled dreams. Such values draw us close to Him. But when our pursuit is for our *will to be done*, then it's no longer something that draws us close to Him. Instead, it competes with Him.

In revival praying I return to verses like Second Chronicles 7:14. They are the bedrock of such cries: *"And My people who are called by My name humble themselves and pray and seek My face and turn from their wicked ways, then I will hear from heaven, will forgive their sin and will heal their land"* (2 Chron. 7:14). This provides us with some of the clearest instructions in the entire Bible about prayer and the potential impact of partnering with God for transformation.

1. Humble themselves.

2. Pray.

3. Seek His face.

4. Turn from wicked ways.

This kind of praying has the entire globe in mind.

Notice first that the people of God are the ones who have the responsibility to pray. Not the sinners. We often think if only those sinners would repent, things would change. Our Father makes it clear it's up to us. Such a prayer must come from humility and be set on one thing—the face of God. Seeking the countenance of a perfect Father speaks to the nature of our prayer assignment in profound ways. If He is revealed on the faces of those who seek Him, and only Him, salvation comes to the nations. (See Psalm 67.) Secondly, there must be a turning away from any known sin through confession and repentance. Thirdly, God forgives us, but He also heals our land. There is a natural healing of land that takes place in this verse, as has been seen in different parts of the world. Almolonga, Guatemala, is one brilliant example.[7] Creation longs for us to live righteously, as is seen in Psalm 67:6. But the healing of the land can also include restoring a nation to its original design and plan. Many of God's works touch both the natural and the spiritual. The man at the gate beautiful was healed physically and walked. But he also praised God, identifying a spiritual healing as well. We need this in our lands—natural and spiritual restoration to our original design and purpose.

THE SACRIFICE ON THE ALTAR

Evan Roberts is a familiar name for anyone who has read about the Welsh Revival of the early 1900s. He is one of my favorite historical figures, especially as it pertains to revival. He was so unassuming and, in many respects, unqualified to be a leader in the great move of God in a nation known for revival. He was too young and way too inexperienced. But perhaps that's what qualified him. He knew what he didn't know and would have to depend on God for the simplest directions and ideas.[8]

Dependency on God is often taken for granted as we become more experienced in the things of God. It becomes too easy to assume we know what to do in a given moment, when in fact, God is wanting to do something new. Doing a new thing with seasoned saints is a rare occurrence in Church history. In our efforts to be good leaders we have the tendency to "skate to where the puck is going." This insightful leadership quote by the renowned hockey player, Wayne Gretzky, addresses one of his keys to greatness. Things are different in revival, as one of our strengths soon becomes our greatest weakness. God is looking for great followers, out of whom to make a new kind of leader. In *skating to where the puck is going,* one has to presume to know where God is going. The very fact that oftentimes God is wanting to do a new thing alerts us to this fact—we don't know what He's about to do.

God is looking for great followers,
out of whom to make a new kind of leader.

But what grabs my attention are the prayers of Evan Roberts that preceded the revival. He once heard Seth Joshua, a great leader in the Church of Wales, pray this prayer, "Bend me." Evan adopted that prayer as his own, and it became the cry that ushered in a nation-changing era.

That's got to be one of the simplest prayers ever prayed. And yet it moved God deeply because it came as an expression of surrender to God and His purposes on earth. In this prayer Evan put himself on the altar.

Once again, a pattern is given to us for revival prayers. While I don't believe in formulas for something of this magnitude, I do believe that certain Kingdom values and principles are unchanging. Evan believed he received directions from the Lord about how to cultivate an atmosphere where the Holy Spirit would be welcomed.

1. We must confess before God every sin in our past life that has not been confessed.

2. We must remove anything that is doubtful in our lives.

3. Total Surrender. We must say and do all that the Spirit tells us.

4. Make a public confession of Christ.[9]

FOLLOW THE CLOUD

In the Kingdom of God, great leaders are measured by their ability to follow.

Israel's wilderness experience offers many lessons to us that can assist us in this revival endeavor. The most obvious is their need to follow the cloud.

The cloud was a manifestation of the presence of God over them as a people. This cloud became a fire by night, but was a protective covering by day. The challenging part for them was the fact that there were times that the cloud would begin to move and they had to pack up their things quickly and follow the cloud. Their entire life was connected to the cloud, the presence. Provision, safety, direction, purpose, and so much more were connected to God Himself, the cloud. To not follow Him meant that all that kept them alive was gone. All the gracious benefits of God's presence just left camp, and to maintain that blessing upon their lives meant they had to go with God.

Revivals challenge us at our very core.

Revivals provide the same challenge. It's not that those who never enter into the new thing that God is doing aren't really saved. I don't believe that at all. But it does mean that person will never experience what God made available for them while still on earth, as revival is always a taste of Heaven in unfathomable ways. Revivals challenge us at our very core.

FOLLOWING OFF THE MAP

History provides us with a lesson from a great military leader. Alexander the Great led his armies in victory after victory, and his desire for ever greater conquest finally brought him to the foot of the Himalayas. He wanted to go beyond these intimidating mountains. Yet, no one knew what was on the other side. Senior officers were troubled by his new vision. Why? They had gone to the edge of their map—there was no map for the new territory that Alexander wanted to possess. These officers had a decision to make: Would they be willing to follow their leader off the map, or would they be content to live within its boundaries? They chose to follow Alexander.

Following the leading of the Holy Spirit can present us with the same dilemma. While he never contradicts His Word, He is very comfortable contradicting our understanding of it. Those who feel safe because of their intellectual grasp of Scriptures enjoy a false sense of security. None of us has a full grasp of Scripture, but we all have the Holy Spirit. He is our common denominator who will always lead us into truth. But to follow Him, we must be willing to follow off the map—to go beyond what we know. To do so successfully we must recognize His presence above all.

There is a great difference between the way Jesus did ministry and the way it typically is done today. He was completely dependent on what the Father was doing and saying. He illustrated this lifestyle after His Holy Spirit baptism. He followed the Holy Spirit's leading, even when it seemed unreasonable, which it often did.

The Church has all too often lived according to an intellectual approach to the Scriptures, void of the Holy Spirit's influence. We have programs and institutions that in no way require the Spirit of God to survive. In fact, much of what we call ministry has no safeguard in it to ensure that He is even present. When our focus is not the presence of God, we end up doing the best we can for God. Our intentions may be noble, but they are powerless in effect. Praying for and living in revival relies completely on the manifest presence of Jesus through the Holy Spirit.[10]

BORN FOR SIGNIFICANCE

When we were born for something more, it becomes inexcusable to be satisfied with anything less. Perhaps our satisfaction with less is in part due to our blindness in reading His Word. It works against the purposes of God for us to read of the great Holy Spirit outpourings in history and assume they were for that day only. They are by nature revelations of His nature, Kingdom, and promises that we might be unsatisfied with where we are. Such a dissatisfaction is not so that we will strategize and plan for the next great move. It's to create in us a great hunger that we might pull into our day all that He has made possible through Christ.

When we were born for something more, it becomes inexcusable to be satisfied with anything less.

NOTES

1. Leonard Ravenhill. *Why Revival Tarries* (Minneapolis: Bethany House Publishers, 2004), 20.

2. I talk of his life more in my book with Jennifer A. Miskov, PhD, *Defining Moments: God-Encounters with Ordinary People Who Changed the World* (New Kensington, PA: Whitaker House, 2016).

3. Charles Grandison Finney, *Memoirs of Reverend Charles G. Finney Written by Himself* (New York: A.S. Barnes, 1876), 13–23.

4. Ibid.

5. Ibid.

6. Ibid.

7. The *Transformations: A Documentary* videos from George Otis Jr. give wonderful insight in this miracle of revival.

8. I talk of his life more in my book with Jennifer A. Miskov, PhD, *Defining Moments: God-Encounters with Ordinary People Who Changed the World* (New Kensington, PA: Whitaker House, 2016).

9. Phillips, *Evan Roberts,* 215. From a letter dated November 5, 1904. See also Shaw, *Great Revival in Wales,* 67-68.

10. Taken from Bill Johnson, *When Heaven Invades Earth.* (Shippensburg, PA: Destiny Image Publishers, 2005), Chapter 6.

Chapter Six

THE KEY
TO REVIVAL

Revival is a renewed conviction of sin and repentance,
followed by an intense desire to live in obedience to
God. It is giving up one's will to God in deep humility.
—CHARLES FINNEY

THERE are times when we do things out of raw obedience, without any emotion, whatsoever. It's not bad or wrong. In fact, it is an important and necessary part of discipleship. Sometimes raw obedience is the purist evidence of our being real followers of Jesus. Every believer must learn to do what is right, because it is right. Period. But having a marriage that is entirely focused on raw obedience, doing the right thing, going through the motions without any affection or interaction, eventually gets old and undesirable. It's not Christlike as a lifestyle. Jesus had more joy than all of His disciples combined. (See Hebrews 1:9.) In Paul's definition of the Kingdom of God— *righteousness, peace, and joy*—two thirds (peace and joy) of the Kingdom are felt realities. (See Romans 14:17.) While we will have situations where we are to give our all, even when there's no feeling to back it up, we are never to settle for that as a lifestyle. Passion and affection are notable expressions consistent with following Jesus.

I've already stated my agreement that the most necessary catalyst to revival is prayer. But at this point I'd like to add a P.S. to that statement: The one thing that enhances prayer to a supernatural level is hunger. Society is more inclined to forgive a thief if he steals to feed his family. And while he must restore what was taken, there is a societal grace for that man because of his drive: He was hungry. We also know that unrighteous people become righteous because of their hunger for righteousness. In the Sermon on the Mount Jesus speaks of this hunger with honor, saying *"they shall be filled."* (See Matthew 5:6.) This word *filled* is often used to describe the fattening of an animal. In other words, we are filled with abundance. Hunger alone accesses that kind of abundance.

Revival praying then is generally filled with prayers of passion, abandonment, and absolute surrender. These expressions are irreplaceable in the context of pursuing revival. But if you don't have that kind of stirring going on inside of you, pray out of raw obedience until you do. Just be honest, and invite God to give you His heart in the matter. That willingness to obey attracts the hand of God in powerful ways. It's also good to note for those lacking passion that you can't interact with Him for long and not pick up His heart. He burns for us with unbridled passion. Even His eyes, that are fixed on us, burn with fire.

A key to revival, then, is not the prayer of duty, where we recite prayers because it's the right thing to do. It is the hunger-driven cries of the heart that will not be satisfied with anything less than an ever-deepening encounter with the Almighty God. That, in essence, is revival.

DESIGNED FOR HUNGER

Becoming hungry is really not that hard. It is our nature in Christ. It is equally true that is in our new nature to believe God, to have faith.

We often live overly aware of the old nature so much that we shut down the reality of who we are in Christ, and who He is in us. *"Therefore if anyone is in Christ, he is a new creature; the old things passed away; behold, new things have come"* (2 Cor. 5:17). It is not a vain imagination to see ourselves as a new creation. In fact, it is the new logic. Paul put it this way, *"Knowing that Christ, having been raised from the dead, is never to die again . . . even so consider yourselves to be dead to sin, but alive to God in Christ Jesus"* (Rom. 6:9-11). The resurrection of Jesus, who will never die again, is the basis for the reality that I am dead to sin. I am to think of myself in this way because of His resurrection. They are equal realities.

But if I have more input from mainstream media than I do from the Word of God and the testimony of the Lord, then my discouragement and lack of focus are my own doing. I have mandated a worldly view by my self-imposed feeding ritual. You are what you eat. And when we feed on the inferior realities of this world, we cannot be surprised that we fall short of the Kingdom lifestyle we've been invited into.

If I have more input from mainstream media than I do from the Word of God and the testimony of the Lord, then my discouragement and lack of focus are my own doing.

CREATING PERSONAL HUNGER

If you lack hunger for revival, acknowledge it before God. Shame won't help, so avoid that at all costs. Thinking happy thoughts is not the cure either. The blood of Jesus in the only answer. And confession connects us to the cleansing provided for by His forgiveness. (See 1 John 1:9.) Confession is powerful and highly valued by God. It's valuable because it basically means we agree with Him. He points to a sin, and we agree by confessing what He pointed to. Returning to the Word of God is next. Probably most of you don't need to return, as you never left it. Yet many read out of ritual, and not for encounter. The Word of God in print is to lead us to the Word of God in Spirit. He is a living person. That's not to discount the printed Word, as it is the living heart of God released to bring transformation to the individual. Just read to obtain.

The Word of God in print is to lead us to the Word of God in Spirit.

Specifically, read about the transformation of Nineveh, one of the greatest miracles in the Bible, found in the Book of Jonah. A whole city, in fact an entire empire, repented. The prophet didn't even tell Nineveh to repent. They simply discovered that the hand of God was against them, and they sought Him for mercy. God's heart was so tender oward them that He forgave them and healed their land. They weren't Jews. They were heathen. And yet God gave them something that would become common in the New Testament. Meditate on that, then consider the sin-filled cities of the world and which ones you think God would like to visit in that way.

Read of the story of the transformation that took place in Ephesus, addressed in Acts 19. This is where Paul broke into *extraordinary miracles*. That's amazing, as apparently miracles had become normal, and it was time for the increased level of breakthrough that Jesus promised when He said, *"Truly, truly, I say to you, he who believes in Me, the works that I do, he will do also; and greater works than these he will do; because I go to the Father"* (John 14:12). This reality of *greater works* started to take place in Ephesus. People touched Jesus' garment and became healed. In Acts 19, they took articles of clothing from Paul's body and laid them on people with disease or demons, and they were healed/delivered. Here they didn't come to Paul. His clothing went to them. *Greater works!* Should these kinds of miracles and city transformations be happening today? See it. Pray it!

Prayerfully study Jesus' warning to the cities most familiar with His ministry:

> *Woe to you, Chorazin! Woe to you, Bethsaida! For **if the miracles** had occurred in Tyre and Sidon which occurred in you, **they would have repented** long ago in sackcloth and ashes . . . and you, Capernaum, will not be exalted to heaven, will you? You will descend to Hades; for **if the miracles** had occurred in Sodom which occurred in you, **it would have remained** to this day* (Matthew 11:21-23).

Historically, the sin-filled cities mentioned in this passage have become the ultimate illustration of debauchery and evil. In Scripture, just the mention of their names evoked a context of evil that was unsurpassed in history. And yet Jesus made a startling statement here, one that should trouble every believer, that these worst of the worst would have repented, and as a result would still be among us as the great cities of the world.

Dreaming what God dreams of connects us to our purpose and destiny. Hunger is not a problem in that context. It's natural. And yet there are still many that have been buried in bad teaching that even surpasses the devastating words and practices of the Pharisees. The religious leaders of Jesus' day were guilty of speaking truth but not living it. Today's Pharisees contradict the truth by cancelling what Jesus taught and practiced. "Miracles are not for today, and if you pursue them you work against Christ!" To believe such nonsense, you have to remove the commissions Jesus gave His disciples and cancel His promises and His pronounced purpose for our becoming full of the Holy Spirit, which is a biblical command. And while they often point to a group of people that got it wrong to justify their beliefs, you have to leave the Gospel as Jesus taught and practiced it to get that outcome. Sometimes, it takes a while for someone raised in the environment to become hungry according to God's design. While wrong teaching has removed many from the front lines of the battle, disappointment is probably a greater enemy to revival. Even greater than wrong teaching. I deal with this subject much more thoroughly in my book *Strengthen Yourself in the Lord*. But suffice it to say, surrender your disappointment to God, and become renewed in hope again. Don't stop pursuing Him until your heart overflows with hope. Come to grips with the fact that your being filled with hope is no one else's responsibility. My hope is my own responsibility.

One of the most important things you can do to become hungry is to read about past revivals. Let me put it another way: Hunger is created whenever we expose ourselves to the miraculous testimonies of God's supernatural invasions throughout history. The testimony prophesies hope and hunger into the human heart. I remember a pastor friend who, when he finished reading Rick Joyner's book on the Welsh Revival, called *World Aflame,* couldn't stay in his office or home. He went into the woods to pray. Something was exploding in him that could not be contained in a proper setting. It had to be expressed.

My hope is my own responsibility.

There are many great books on revival, ones that tell the stories of the miracle workings of God in the transformation of people and cities. Testimonies prophesy. It is nearly impossible to read these stories and not get hungry. In fact, we don't even think about our need to be hungrier for God, for out of our innermost being comes a cry, almost volcanic in nature, for *more of God at any price.* The prayer that comes forth is not rehearsed. Nor is it written down. It is also not a rote prayer done that we might check it off the list. It is the prayer, manifesting hunger and passion, that only a Father of promises could inspire.

I have witnessed people who had zero hunger for the outpouring of the Holy Spirit, who witnessed a miracle in their own life, or even with a close friend, and were ignited in a moment. One pastor came to me after experiencing a creative miracle in his body that was undeniable. We both actually watched it happen over a period of about 30 seconds. In response, he told me, *"I don't believe what I just saw."* He was serious. He walked around dazed for a good half hour. After the significance of his miracle impacted his heart and mind, he came back to me and said, *"I have discovered why I'm alive."* That night a fiery passion was born. Not the short-lived emotional burst. But the kind that is anchored in our purpose for being.

WISE MEN STILL TRAVEL

I've heard people say, more times than I care to remember, "God knows we want revival. If it's His will, He'll cause it to happen. He knows where we live." I'm sure the intentions are good. But that kind of praying violates so much of His heart and nature that it's scary. We have the responsibility to pursue Him. He's not the cosmic bell hop looking for a way to please us. He is a loving Father, for sure, but He remains the sovereign Lord over all, who longs for partnership with those who have received His Son Jesus. Scripture calls it *co-laboring*.

He has given us His promises and a covenantal agreement to meet us when we seek Him. While He knows what we need before we ask, He requires us to ask, even for our daily bread. It's not that He doesn't know or remember. It's that He longs for us to pursue Him, mindful of His covenant and promises. Aligning with His Word is essential in learning to apprehend all that He has made available in this life. Most of what we need in this life will be brought to us. But most of what we want we'll have to go get. The pursuit is needed for our sakes. It is in the pursuit that we demonstrate great faith in His Word and covenant. Plus, the pursuit changes us into the kind of disciple that will better steward the answer once it comes.

I realize that not everyone can afford to go around the world. But you might be surprised what He will fund if the hunger is in place. Pursue Him and His work with all you have, and He will provide for everything that He inspires that takes deep root in our hearts.

Most of what we need in this life will be brought to us. But most of what we want we'll have to go get.

Having said that, we must be willing to go wherever God is moving. I have traveled extensively in pursuit of all that God is doing. It started with conferences in which my heroes of the faith were ministering. Jack Hayford and John Wimber, for example. My hunger also took me to Toronto, Pensacola, Pasadena, St. Louis, Spokane, Wales, Argentina, and many other places just to see what God was doing. But not merely as an observer. I long to be in the middle of whatever He is doing. I just want to be a yielded participant.

HONORING GENERALS

Many years ago, God impressed upon my heart that we needed to honor those who have gone before us, even those whose lives ended in failure. If we did as He commanded, He would release to us the gifts and anointings of those who have gone before us. In the Kingdom of God, much of what we receive is given to us in the same measure of the honor we give. Jesus addressed the principle with, *"A prophet is not without honor except in his hometown and in his own household"* (Matt.13:57). So, I've made it my mission for many years to honor the generals of the past, even to the point of being careful of how I talk about them and their failures.

I don't mean we are to ignore or hide their sins. God doesn't do that in the Bible. But neither should any of us take delight in discussing them, as though we are superior in any way. That is a sure sign that we have a blindness to our own weaknesses. Without repentance, that can only lead to one thing—personal failure.

I've even gone to the gravesites of great revivalists, like Smith Wigglesworth, Charles Finney, John G. Lake, and Evan Roberts, just to pray. And in spite of the rumors, I do not go to talk to the dead or ask for anything from them. I go to the gravesite to honor God for the great things He did through their surrender, as imperfect as they may have been. For me these sites are like the memorial stones of the Old Testament, which were physical reminders to the Jewish people of their miraculous history with God. In the same way, these memorial stones are to remind us of what is possible through one yielded life. When I stand near their grave, I remind God of what they accomplished in His name, reciting their words or actions to Him. It is my effort to join my heart to the way God touched and used them in a mighty way. And then I ask God to do it again and include me in what He's doing. I've had great affection stir up in my heart for the heroes of the past and overwhelming thankfulness that He would use us in a way that honors Him and honors those who paved the way for us to have the opportunities we presently have.

PROVERBS AND REVIVAL

It is my personal conviction that revival starts with power, but is sustained through wisdom. I hope to make that clear throughout this book, as the need of the hour is for both power and wisdom in order to obtain and sustain all that God intends to do in our lifetime.

Revival starts with power,

but is sustained through wisdom.

The Book of Proverbs gives us wisdom and insight for stewarding anything that God gives us, be it money, friends, family, business, or even revival. It's really all about stewardship. I read a chapter a day of this fabulous book, according to the date. Proverbs provides us with brilliant insights that are unparalleled in the rest of Scripture. As a result, they have a place in the complete study of the great moves of God.

The primary focus of Proverbs, and thus the focus of wisdom, is to enable us to reign in life. That doesn't mean to reign over people, in some *we're-better-than-others* approach to life. It's that in wisdom we learn to represent the Lord well in reigning over the issues of life that so many others stumble over. For example, money doesn't control me; I control money for the glory of God.

I will admit that these principles apply to many things other than the great moves of God. My suggestion is that you read this book of wisdom as it pertains to anything God has given you to give oversight or input to. My point is that we also steward revival. Here's one of my favorite verses in this regard.

> *A sated man loathes honey, but to a famished man any bitter thing is sweet* (Proverbs 27:7).

This statement is so profound in its application to the subject of revival that I am amazed that it wasn't the primary purpose of the verse. People who are full (sated) can even despise good things. Satisfied people are poor judges of what God is doing. They don't have a need or appetite for what God is doing. Not really. Hunger and the recognition of personal need are the most trusted interpreters of the moves of God. The prostitute, thief, and demonized recognized Him when He came. Why? They lived aware of their need.

But the religious leaders in Jesus' day didn't. Amazingly, what is *sweet* to everyone else in the room is distasteful to them. In fact, this kind of person becomes the restaurant critic, or dare I say *revival critic*. They point to countless expressions of revival, always criticizing them, saying, "That's not revival." I remember one guy declaring those words to me. Here is my thought, "I don't know what's happening in that three-foot circle you're standing in, but in this one, I am burning with the fire of revival." Take responsibility for your own experience, your own fire. Isn't that the lesson of the ten virgins in Matthew 25? Five made sure they had oil for their lamps to burn, and the five foolish ran out of oil as they didn't take personal responsibility. Make certain the fire is burning in you, it's burning brightly, and there's enough oil for all your days here on earth.

There are more revival critics in this day than I can imagine at any other time in history. I'm certain that it's the use of social media that makes everyone appear to be an expert. What I've learned from the recent invasion of social media into many of our lives is that you no longer need insight or intelligence to have an opinion. And political correctness proves that stupidity is contagious. Wrong values appear to be wisdom. Fear always masquerades as wisdom; otherwise, it would be rejected soundly. It's amazing how fast a lie can spread and anti-Kingdom values can be promoted as the Gospel, and living under the fear of man can be considered a virtue. The state of being deeply rooted in the Word of God and in constant fellowship with the Spirit of God is the two-edged sword that keeps us in continual safety. Walking with people of like mind helps immeasurably in the life of revival. The Word, the Spirit, and the people of God comprise the threefold cord that is not easily broken.

How we live our lives really matters. We're not to be controlled or influenced by what is popular or commonly believed by the masses. Jesus calls us to Himself, to be like Him. We are not culturally relevant when we mirror the culture around us. We are culturally relevant when we model the lifestyle of the Kingdom of God that the world longs to obtain. Everyone wants peace, love, and joy. When we walk in those things, regardless of circumstances, we manifest the nature of His world that cannot be shaken. I remind you: everyone wants a king like Jesus. He is the desire of the nations. *"And I will shake all nations, and the desire of all nations shall come: and I will fill this house with glory, saith the Lord of hosts"* (Hag. 2:7 KJV). We must illustrate what it looks like to thrive in life, regardless of the conditions around us. Many at this point would think I'm referring to money. While I admit it sometimes includes money, the real issue is the prosperity of soul. (See 3 John 2.) How are we doing in our internal world? That is the real issue. In fact, our countenance is the only Gospel that many will ever read.

The psalmist put it this way, *"God be gracious to us and bless us, and cause His face to shine upon us—Selah. That Your way may be known on the earth, Your salvation among all nations"* (Ps. 67:1-2). It's remarkable how realizing God's face of delight over us affects our own countenance. And that becomes our witness. Notice the conclusion of this psalm is the salvation of the nations.

There are different realities, each competing for our attention, and ultimately our affection. There's the power of darkness, filled with fear, anger, bitterness, arrogance, etc. And there's the Kingdom of God, filled with love, joy, and peace. Our countenance will always reflect the nature of the world we are most aware of.

MULTIGENERATIONAL MIGRATION

A few months ago, Beni and I were watching TV together when something grabbed my attention. Actually, I was sort of watching while also playing on my iPad, which is a common habit of mine. In the middle of my iPad experience, I heard this phrase coming from the program: *multigenerational migration.* That phrase grabbed my heart, in a very real sense. I put down my iPad and began to watch, as I sensed something profound and inviting was being spoken. It happened to be a documentary on monarch butterflies, which is not the kind of thing we usually watch together. As I began to listen, I was captured again by the phrase, *multigenerational migration.*

After finishing that program, I went to YouTube and searched this subject. I was able to find many other videos on this subject. It caught my attention for so many reasons, not the least of which is that we intentionally live with an awareness of our multigenerational impact and the responsibility to leave an inheritance. In fact, my son Eric and I co-authored a book on this subject called, *Momentum: What God Starts Never Ends.* It's a theme that has been all important to us and has marked our decisions for many years. But this program introduced me to something I was not aware of. It seemed that there was something in this idea that could possibly help us go to the next level in a move of God.

What the producers of this show wanted us to learn was that monarch butterflies migrate from Mexico to Canada. They showed us the forests in Mexico where around 200 million of these butterflies exist at one time. Once they start their travels, it takes four generations for them to reach their destination. Imagine this: The butterfly leaves the millions of other butterflies that live in a particular forest in Mexico and begins the journey to Canada. When they've traveled their prescribed distance, they lay eggs, which become caterpillars, each of which forms a cocoon, out of which comes a butterfly. Then those fly as far as they can, then laying eggs for the next generation of butterflies to continue the trip. Instinctively, they know their assignments. This is similar to salmon, who travel back to the same river they were born in. But the monarch butterfly has an inbuilt assignment that in some ways is even more impressive than the salmon. For the monarch, it takes four generations to complete what they were born for. Perhaps that's why every believer instinctively longs for more. And once the concept of revival is revealed as a possibility, little else matters. Living with the realization that it will not be one generation that gets our assignment finished might help us as we prepare the next generation for their *reason for being.*

After four generations, the butterflies reach their destiny. And then they start the same trip back to Mexico, which takes another four generations. Is it possible that we fall short in revival because we sell short all that God wants to do? What He has planned can't be accomplished by one generation. Instead, it is to be a cooperative effort of multiple generations. He is the God of Abraham, Isaac, and Jacob, all at the same time. He reigns over the intentions and purposes of multiple generations. One of our main responsibilities is to prepare the following generation, through instruction, example, and opportunity, with the responsibility to live in the spirit of revival all of their days, and to expect nothing less.

What He has planned can't be accomplished by one generation. Instead, it is to be a cooperative effort of multiple generations.

It was the absence of the hunger he once had that took one of the greatest reformers in all of history, King Hezekiah, and stripped him of his multigenerational influence. It happened when he was rebuked by Isaiah for his sin. He then told him that his sons would become eunuchs in the Babylonian empire. King Hezekiah responded that the word was good, because *"at least there will be peace in my days."* (See Isaiah 39:5-8.) Thus, his multigenerational migration ended. He lost sight of his responsibility for long-term influence and settled for enjoying favor in his day, even though the next generation would suffer because of his choices. Hezekiah's reign, one of the greatest in history, was followed by that of his son, Manasseh, one of the evilest kings in history. Whenever we misplace or misuse something God has given us, something inferior always grows in its place.

KEEPING THE MAIN THING THE MAIN THING

We had experienced a mighty outpouring of the Holy Spirit in 1987 that started immediately after several of us attended a Signs and Wonders Conference at the Anaheim Vineyard Church with John Wimber. Several other notable speakers were there. I was deeply touched. And while no one ever prayed for us or prophesied over us, we went home changed and encouraged. The miracles started the next week. To put this in perspective, I had not seen healing or miracles when I prayed although I had taught it and practiced it for years. It just didn't happen. Until now. I didn't pray differently. I didn't teach anything different. Yet Jesus came in ways I had only hoped for. And while we experienced an ever-increasing outpouring for a season, I didn't know how to sustain it. I didn't even know I needed to know how to sustain it. But much like the priests in the Old Testament, I was faced with the reality that a fire goes out when there's no more fuel.

God was so good to us, as the Holy Spirit would come in power at different times throughout the next eight years. They were like waves. It felt like something was missing, as this outpouring never became a way of life. Looking back, I can see that I thought this was God's will for us. I assumed it was His desire for us to experience Him in this way—occasionally. It was His sovereignty. Or so I thought.

In 1995, I decided to visit Toronto, where I heard that God was moving powerfully. And even though much of what happened there was maligned by many, it was worth the risk. On my flight to that great city, I found myself praying, "God, if you touch me again, I'll never change the subject." In praying, I discovered I had a conviction that had not been put into words before, nor had I consciously thought this through. It became apparent to me that in 1987 I had added what God was doing to what we were already doing. My prayer for Him to touch me again included my commitment never to change the subject from what the Father was doing.

When I walked into the auditorium at Toronto Airport Christian Fellowship, I was overwhelmed by the manifestations of 5000 people. It wasn't that I hadn't seen any of it before. It's just that I had only experienced that in small numbers. Five thousand people, all passionate about Jesus, was overwhelming. So, I closed my eyes and turned my affection to the Lord. In that moment I realized what filled that room was the same anointing and presence that we had experienced in some of our late-night prayer meetings back home. Recognizing His presence made it much easier to relax and enjoy this unusual, but *pregnant*, Holy Spirit moment.

When we are in a situation that is new to us and we are trying to discern if it is from God or not, our greatest tool is our ability to recognize Him. Too many conclude that if they feel uncomfortable with something, what they are observing must not be from God. That's not entirely true. He's the comforter. But often where He leads us is challenging, stretching us far beyond our comfort zones. In reality, He leads me to where I need His comfort. There's a big difference between the *warning* that the Holy Spirit gives us when something is false and the discomfort we feel when it is outside our understanding or personal history. Learning the difference is paramount, especially in seasons of mighty outpouring. We must learn the privilege of recognizing Him in our private times with the Lord. What we learn there will always help in the corporate gatherings.

Combined with the ability to recognize the presence of the Holy Spirit, our greatest safeguard against deception is our immersion into the Word of God. And while I know that biblical knowledge is usually the only thing emphasized at this point of the discussion, many who use only that point are the most deceived as it pertains to the moves of God. Again, allow the Word of God to lead you to the person of Jesus Christ. He is to be known, encountered, and completely trusted.

To experience the peace that surpasses understanding, I have to give up my right to understand.

The Holy Spirit brings peace to us when we lack understanding. It's the Bible that elevates this element above understanding, as the heart will take us further in God than the mind ever will. For this reason, Paul teaches that God gives us peace that passes understanding. (See Philippians 4:8.) And that peace takes a military posture of protection of all that pertains to me. Peace protects us where understanding can't. To experience the peace that surpasses understanding, I have to give up my right to understand. Again, it's not that the mind isn't important. It actually is very important. But when my mind runs my Christian life, I have an inferior Christian life. Surrender to the purposes and methods of God is the key to all activity in the Kingdom. Especially, revival.

BLOCKAGES? OR INVITATIONS?

One of the most common sermons I have heard through the years is what we must do if we want revival. Of course, these sermons seldom come from anyone who has ever experienced one. They usually come from people who have read the books on the subject and have great hunger. I applaud them. Together, we will come into the greater things of God for this next season.

This section is where I could unintentionally cause the most offense. But only if you miss the main point of this next section. So please read carefully what is written.

In the following section I'm going to list all the various parts of our lives that are considered blockages to a great move of God. While I support each idea as extremely important, they don't block His coming. He enters the place where He is welcome.

Many people want to become closer to perfect so God will come. It reminds me of the person who cleans their own home before they have the cleaners come and do their job. We try to get ourselves ready for the mighty outpouring by making ourselves worthy. No one would ever put it that way, but it is the reality of this kind of mindset.

Here is a list of very important things I've heard taught as things we must deal with before we can ever expect to have a revival:

- Restore corporate prayer meetings, then we'll have revival.

- Get back to the discipline of prayer with fasting, then we'll have revival.

- Reprioritize the study of the Bible, then we'll have revival.

- Return to honoring and praying for Israel properly, then we'll have revival.

- Make children the priority of the church, then we'll have revival.

- Become compassionate and take care of the poor, then we can have revival.

- Restore honor to the elderly, then we'll have revival.

- We must pursue reconciliation in all our relationships before we can have revival.

- We must learn to prioritize the youth, or we will never have revival.

- We must deal with the issue of systemic racism before we can ever expect revival.

- If we can reject materialism and learn generosity as a lifestyle, then we can have revival.

- Until women are valued and celebrated correctly, we can never expect revival.

- Repent for the breaking of covenants with the First Nations People; then we can have revival.

- If we would only pray more in our personal lives, then we could expect revival.

This list could go on and on, but hopefully you get the point. All of these are extremely important issues for us to give our attention to. They are vital. But God knows us. He knows that if we get all our things in order, and then He comes in power, we'll ultimately take credit for the revival. We sometimes get the cart before the horse, so to speak. What we read in our history books as manifestations of a great move of God, is actually the fruit of revival, not the cause. Now obviously, if God says fast, we fast. Prayer and obedience remain key to being involved in an outpouring of the Holy Spirit. And we should always be asking for more. But we often work so hard to bring about a revival that we bypass the number-one ingredient: Him. Welcoming Him, giving place to His heart, making room in our lives, our day, our services just for Him, is the issue. We work so hard for Him that He could come and we wouldn't know it.

All of these things on my list are vital. You could probably add to the list from your own convictions, or perhaps revival sermons you've heard. The problem is not with the list. The problem is we often mistake what changes in revival, with what we must do to get revival. If He came only after we'd taken care of the things on my list, we'd end up thinking the move of God was about us. And if there's one thing we must learn in this endeavor, it's that God moves in a way where only He receives the glory. Our honor is to participate.

So here is a simple response to some of the issues mentioned above:

> Praying for revival is extremely important. But you'll pray more when revival comes. And the praying we do in revival is in part what sustains it.

Fasting has its place in the pursuit of revival, but you'll fast more and with greater ease once revival comes. Fasting is essentially hungering for something that food cannot satisfy. And no price is too big to continue in the wonder of such a glorious thing as revival.

Giving honor to children, youth, and elderly are vital expressions of the Christian life. It is normal Christianity. But then so is revival. We do everything better and naturally in revival.

Materialism is idolatry. But materialism ceases in revival, as nothing else matters. Even the early Church, while in the throes of revival, considered nothing as belonging to themselves as they sought how to live generous lifestyles. (See Acts 4:32.)

There is no excuse for the abuses and broken covenants given to our First Nations People. One of the first things we did in the outpouring of the Holy Spirit among us was to honor our local tribe with words of affirmation, prayer, and financial support once revival came. It is the fruit, not the cause.

The lingering effects of slavery inspire an insidious attitude of superiority that gives way to the spirit of racism. Racism in all its forms, is evil to its core. Revival is life in the glory. Jesus said He gave us His glory that we might be one. (See John 17:22.) Unity, even racial unity, is best accomplished in the glory, which is a manifestation of revival.

The point is, whatever you think needs to be fixed before He comes in power is probably what He wants to fix in His coming. If He says fast for three days, and then He'll come in power, do it. Pure and simple. But we need to stop trying to earn the favor He has given us and learn to welcome Him into every single part of our lives. This is a relational journey, which means we are constantly dealing with whatever He addresses in that journey.

HUNGER, THE GIFT FROM GOD

To conclude, hunger is a good sign. I am an extremely happy parent of three children. Each of them married godly spouses, who have in turn given Beni and me 11 grandchildren. Being a parent, and watching them grow up into God's design for them is one of the greatest privileges we can enjoy this side of Heaven. But I remember well when they were infants. One of the ways you could tell when one of them was sick was they lost their hunger. Of course, there are fevers and other manifestations of sickness. But the one that still influences my thinking to this day is the absence of hunger. That is a sign of sickness. This is absolutely true for the followers of Jesus. The absence of hunger speaks to the heart condition that needs reviving. It needs to be warmed by the love of God that restores hope and our connection to why we're alive.

In the same way that we can't crave something sweet unless *sweet* exists, we can't hunger for the reality of Heaven on earth unless that reality exists. Revival is such a reality. We know it exists as it was seen in Jesus' lifestyle. We also know it is within reach because Jesus taught us to pray for it through the following Disciples' Prayer:

> *Our Father who is in heaven,*
> *Hallowed be Your name.*
> ***Your kingdom come.***
> ***Your will be done,***

On earth as it is in heaven.
Give us this day our daily bread.
And forgive us our debts, as we also have forgiven our debtors.
And do not lead us into temptation, but deliver us from evil.
For Yours is the kingdom and the power and the glory forever.
Amen (Matthew 6:9-13).

We were designed for eternity in Heaven. It is our nature to hunger for that reality now, through the various manifestations of revival and His many displays of glory. Revival is living in the glory.

Chapter Seven

SPIRITUAL RICHES

A genuine revival without joy in the Lord is as
impossible as spring without flowers,
or day-dawn with light.
—CHARLES SPURGEON

THERE is a principle found throughout the Scriptures that actually has a greater effect on the subject of revival than most any of us would have thought. It is *first the natural, then the spiritual*. Our stewardship of natural things prepares us for the stewardship of the spiritual. The apostle Paul coined this phrase in his instruction to the church at Corinth. He was teaching them about the mystery and necessity of the resurrection.

> *However, the spiritual is not first, but the natural; then the*
> *spiritual* (1 Corinthians 15:46).

To illustrate the concept as it appears through Scripture, a natural lamb was sacrificed for the atonement of sin. Jesus, the eternal Lamb of God came upon the scene to fulfill all requirements of the law on our behalf by giving Himself as an offering. In doing so, He did away with animal sacrifices. *First the natural* lamb, *then the spiritual* lamb.

First the natural, then the spiritual.

Our stewardship of natural things prepares us

for the stewardship of the spiritual.

And again, Adam was the father of humanity. Had he lived in righteousness, it would have been our inheritance to this day. But instead, he sinned, and we inherit the sad consequences of that wrong. Jesus came as the sinless last Adam, becoming the *"everlasting father"* of a whole new kind of people called a *"chosen race"* in First Peter 2:9. And in the same way as we all inherited a fallen world through the first Adam, so we can inherit by the righteousness of Christ in our last Adam a redeemed revival of His Kingdom through our own surrender to Him. *First the natural* Adam, *then the spiritual* Adam.

This concept runs through the whole of Scripture. But Jesus taught this principle in a most unusual—and in today's climate— highly offensive way. He used the concept as it pertains to money.

> *Therefore if you have not been faithful in the use of unrighteous wealth, who will entrust the true riches to you? And if you have not been faithful in the use of that which is another's, who will give you that which is your own?* (Luke 16:11-12).

"True riches" does not mean more money. He was not teaching how to increase your income or better yourself as it pertains to your financial

security. The lesson isn't *if you handle money well, you will get more of it*. There are other places in the Bible that give us insight about bringing increase into our lives in general, whether it's finances, use of the gifts, friendships, etc. But here, He states quite plainly that the level of our faithfulness in the use of unrighteous money determines the measure of the *true riches* we will enjoy. True riches are not of this world. It is the realm of the Kingdom of God, manifested upon our lives, that is the crowning touch to our faithful stewardship of money. For me, "true riches" easily addresses the subject of revival, for the manifest presence of God, His revealed glory and the absolute downpour of the Holy Spirit is the ultimate example of true riches.

The outpouring of the Holy Spirit is Heaven's greatest wealth, called *presence*, being poured out upon a most needy people. I don't know that we could possibly imagine a greater example of true riches than the Holy Spirit Himself.

CAN'T BE BOUGHT

It would be a grave error to teach that we give unholy money to obtain heavenly riches. There were times in history believers were taught that they could buy salvation for another by their donations to the Church. I hear some leaders teach that if we give them money, God will reward us by healing our sick relative or give us increased anointing in our lives. It is nauseating to read of such things in Church history, let alone to see it happening today. It is an unfortunate reality, both past and present.

We cannot buy healing, revival, or a spiritual refreshing or outpouring of any kind. That is a sick interpretation of this very wonderful truth. And yet what Jesus taught would get Him slandered in today's media with our present political climate. It's important to see the two things Jesus wanted us to experience as results of following His teaching. One is that we would increase in *true riches*, which is not money. Real wealth is the reality of the unseen world, functioning in our lives in a way that glorifies God and further establishes us in identity and purpose. The unseen world is superior in every way to what we see in the natural. And yet it's our care and stewardship over the natural that readies us for the unseen. The second part of this passage has another target, *that which is your own*. Jesus never said money was the root of all evil. It is the love of money that is the root of all evil. Jesus never taught that material things are evil or owning them is wrong. In fact, He promised to bring increase to those areas if we're faithful. (See Mark 10:29-31.) But the target unmistakably is the reality of Heaven on earth. True riches.

THE REALMS OF FINANCIAL TESTING

There are so many aspects of our lives that are in some way connected to money. Money is probably one of the most misunderstood areas of life, and therefore is prone to erroneous teaching on the subject. The two extremes I see are *your spirituality is measured by your income, wealth, possessions, or title.* The second is that *your spirituality is measured by lack, or poverty.* In some ways it's a lot easier to give everything away, then let others face the challenge of proper management of resources, and not us. Such management brings us to the subject of stewardship, which is one of the most vital in all of Scripture. But let me make something very clear here at the onset: Managing money well is seldom about money. Stewardship of money reveals in the natural how well we are managing our thoughts, ambitions, and dreams. It has everything to do with a key verse for my life found in Proverbs 4:23:

Watch over your heart with all diligence,
For from it flow the springs of life.

Stewardship of money reveals in the

natural how well we are managing our

thoughts, ambitions, and dreams.

All the issues of our lives flow from our hearts. The picture is much like a spring in the ground that bubbles up continually, creating various streams that fill the landscape. Managing the heart, the source of that spring, insures the purity of the streams that go out from there to define the life for that individual. On one hand the heart can be known for impurity. Jesus spoke of that reality in this way:

> *For out of the heart come evil thoughts, murders, adulteries, fornications, thefts, false witness, slanders. These are the things which defile the man* (Matthew 15:19-20).

On the complete opposite end of the spectrum, He said:

> *Blessed are the pure in heart, for they shall see God* (Matthew 5:8).

So then, the heart is capable of revealing two completely different realities, two different worlds: the world of spiritual darkness and death or the world of life and true Christlikeness. The choice of the latter is rewarded by seeing the most wonderful and beautiful thing in existence: God Himself. The heart set on seeking the face of God will be rewarded. It is a mockery of God to think we can sow a life of pursuing God and not be rewarded. (See Galatians 6:7.)

Perhaps this one statement helps to clarify this issue for all of us, *"For where your treasure is, there your heart will be also"* (Matt. 6:21). Hearts reveal what we treasure or value most.

STEWARDSHIP

There are four areas of stewardship that stand out to me. I don't intend to make this about money. And even if I reference our financial lives, it is always unto something else, something much more significant and important.

— Giving —

Generosity is a significant part of our life of godly stewardship. I personally still hold to the concept of the tithe as the beginning place of our financial lives, as it is demonstration of our yielding to His Lordship. Many make the mistake of assuming that the Old Testament Law brought about the concept of the tithe. It didn't. It merely ratified what Abraham, the father of faith, first introduced, four hundred years before the Law. Regardless of your convictions, generosity remains a critical part of our lives. But generosity goes far beyond money. It is the ability and desire to express kindness to a waitress, the patience shown in getting our car repaired, or the heart of compassion for the single mom who has fallen on even harder times. It's not a switch that we turn on and off. It is a way of life.

— Contentment —

The more we think our success in life is measured by possessions or income, the more we will slowly sell our soul for increase. And while I seriously mean the phrase, *sell your soul,* it's not a one-time decision to sell out. It is usually a slow burn, in that the passion for wealth begins to rob our soul of its desire for heavenly things. This is very significant in the overall subject of revival, as all significant revivals usher in a time of financial prosperity. It is a reward for seeking first the Kingdom of God. The inability to make that distinction between what we are to pursue, versus the reward for the right pursuit, has cost previous generations the impact on the nations that the momentum of their revival had created. *"Put a knife to your throat if you are a man of great appetite"* (Prov. 23:2). Do whatever you need to do to allow God to bring His intended increase into your life. It is for the purpose of revealing His glory upon His children. But make sure, if you have a *bent* to lust after things, take measures to enforce *self-imposed restrictions.* Such restrictions could save your life.

— Investing —

Here's an apparent contradiction: Not to want more, for the purposes of revealing the glory of God and serving humanity, is to live a self-centered life. How can I hear the cry of the single mom, or the man out of work, or the homeless man by the freeway, and not instinctively want to meet their need? I can't fix every problem around me. But with more resources, I can do more than I am now.

The Bible addresses how to have a healthy family because God wants us to have healthy families. In the same way, the Bible addresses how to bring increase into our lives financially, because He wants us to have increase. God gave seed for sowing because He created the concept of increase. One kernel of corn planted into the ground does not bring a return of one kernel of corn. It wouldn't be worth the effort. It brings a return with significant increase. Two of Jesus' parables deal with God's perspective on increase in profound ways: the parable of the talents and the parable of the minas. Both talents and minas are currency, specific sums of money. In both stories, the persons that were rewarded brought increase. And the only one that was judged in the story was the one who had no increase. Perhaps the strangest part of the story, that is the most offensive to many, is that Jesus took the one talent away from the one unfaithful servant and gave it to the one who had the most. In doing so, Jesus disqualified Himself as a socialist. Of course, these parables speak to areas of life that are not financial in nature. But as I stated earlier, the money part of our lives is the tip of the iceberg, representing much more significant areas that reveal our heart. First the natural, then the spiritual. Our stewardship of money should include the study of bringing about biblical increase in a way that glorifies God and enables us to have greater impact on the world around us.

— Wise Purchases —

We live in a material world that in itself is not evil. While it has certainly been marked by sin and has become the pursuit of those who fall into horrible idolatry/materialism, it is not inherently dark or worldly. Those who laid down what they owned for the purposes of Christ are rewarded with more of what they laid down. (See Mark 10:30.) Jesus included in a concept in the Luke 16 passage mentioned above something I don't think

I've ever heard taught: *"Who will give you that which is your own?"* The concept He deals with here is our willingness to manage, in a responsible way, something that belongs to someone else. It could be a rented car, or the good news of the promotion of a friend or perhaps the tools that your neighbor loaned you; these are all possessions that belong to another. Caring for the rented car like it was my own is my responsibility. It reveals *how much more of my* own I can handle. Rejoicing for my friend who received a promotion at work, sometimes the very promotion I was hoping for, is the test to see if I'm capable of stewarding well *that which is my own*. Returning the borrowed tools, cleaner and better than they were when they were borrowed, often becomes the measure in which I can manage tools of my own. The inescapable point is that God set us up, through godly stewardship, to have something to call our own—increase. He's a good Father, who longs to reward the faithfulness of His children. I believe it is possible to illustrate God's values for excellence and beauty through what we buy, manage, and give oversight to. It was certainly a part of the witness that Solomon had with the Queen of Sheba. (See First Kings 10:1-10.) And it has to be more than just expensive; if not, only the rich could participate. For me it is thoughtful living, with purpose and intentionality, with the goal of always living with excellence. My parents modeled this for me, even when we had very little finances or possessions. For them it was always about being excellent. It's a part of our faith that gets overlooked, as it is a very practical way of illustrating our love for God. *"And whatever you do, do it heartily, as to the Lord"* (Col. 3:23 KJV).

MATERIALISM

When I said yes to following Jesus, I gave Him everything. I didn't care if I ever owned anything more than the clothes on my back and my Bible. Everything else was a bonus. And while giving all is the normal

Christian life, attitudes can be formed that are not Christlike at all. I started to look down on anyone who owned much. My concern about materialism in the Church was legitimate. It has robbed so many of their destiny, causing them to settle for the inferior. Materialism is related to greed, which is called idolatry. (See Ephesians 5:5.) It's no small matter. But I soon learned that if the enemy can't get me to fall in the issue of greed and idolatry, he'll try to get me to fall to a critical spirit toward anyone who owns much. To do so I must assume that they are materialistic and idolatrous, when it could be that they are the ones the Bible talks about, who gave in secret, and God decided to reward them openly. (See Matthew 6:3-4.)

If the enemy can't get me to fall in the issue of greed and idolatry, he'll try to get me to fall to a critical spirit toward anyone who owns much.

I had a view, that is all too common in the Church: despising the natural world. And while I know that creation has been marked by sin, it is still beautiful. According to Paul, we have been given the world, and we have responsibility to care for it.

When I become critical and judgmental of others, I mirror the sin I've accused them of, only worse. It's a trap whenever we think we know the heart of another. We must see this as forbidden territory and simply not go there.

The point is, material things matter in that they are often the canvas upon which we display our commitment to excellence and beauty. It is really possible to reveal the nature of the wisdom of God by stewardship. The material world is also where our standards of stewardship are revealed.

Excellence, creativity, and integrity make up the threefold cord of wisdom. God's nature and goodness can be revealed in what we own and how we steward our possessions. I hold to what I have been entrusted with lightly. The Father will sometimes test our hearts by directing us to give away what is important to us. My priorities of spiritual things are to be revealed by the fact that while I may own things, things don't own me.

We had a season in our married life when almost everything we owned came to us in a very significant way. God provided for us in unusual ways, almost always connected to a moment of challenging obedience that God honored. What is beautiful about that season is the fact my home is filled with what the Bible would call *monuments*: things that testify of God's goodness. When life is lived that way, even the material world speaks of God, stirring our affections for Him, not the inferior.

Stewarding natural blessings reminds me a lot of the challenge Moses had when the Lord told him to throw down his rod. It turned into a snake. And then God told him to pick up the snake by the tail. Doing it the way God said is what kept him from being bitten by that snake. Holding onto God's provision, His way, is what keeps us from being bitten by that snake.

THEN THE SPIRITUAL

When I settle for possessions and positions, in the place of the increase of the unseen realm in my life, I settle for the inferior. The enemy wants me to live in continual distraction so that my affections are misplaced and diluted. Even in my best stewardship of natural things, it is unto something. It is unto spiritual riches, blessings, experiences, insights, and breakthroughs. This is what we were born for. Despising natural things does nothing to prepare me for Heaven.

I know that the way I steward what God has given me is a test for true riches of Kingdom realities. This is an endless list to me: spiritual gifts, promises, favor, insights and revelation, promotion, greater anointing, chances to partner in the impossible, and on and on it goes. The point is, our stewardship of the simple, the natural, is the test for what we can be trusted with in the supernatural. And it is for the supernatural lifestyle that I was born.

Our stewardship of the simple, the natural,

is the test for what we can be trusted

with in the supernatural.

Chapter Eight

KEEPING THE FIRE BURNING

A constant revival state in a congregation is certainly
vastly preferable to temporary excitements, however deep
and beneficial in the results; and if its attainment is
possible, ought not every congregation to enjoy it?
—SIMEON WELCHER HARKEY[1]

I MAKE some people nervous when I teach on anything to do with the sovereignty of God. Because those concerns come from very respected people, consider what I have to say carefully in light of Scripture and *eat the meat and throw out the bones*. Admittedly, my emphasis is generally on our responsibilities before God. Never is it my intention to question or challenge God's nature or heart or what He can and cannot do. He is the sovereign Lord over all. He can do whatever He wants without ever having to explain Himself to any of us. He owes me nothing, yet He gives me everything!

My bigger concern and focus are on our responsibility to do our part in carrying out His sovereign plan. I just don't want to fall short in embracing the assignment He has given to me. In other words, I don't want to be found waiting for Him to do something when He is waiting for me. In my way of thinking, that is the greater concern.

I don't want to be found waiting for Him to do something when He is waiting for me.

Sometimes an unnecessary controversy arises over the subject of God's sovereignty in that there are two realities that need not be in conflict. One is the absolute sovereignty of God, where He is able to act completely separately from our will or desire. We do not control Him at all. The second is that, at the same time, He welcomes us into a relationship where by His design we have the privilege to influence Him. That is the basic privilege of prayer. He can do anything He wants, with or without us. But often He chooses to act in partnership with those made in His image, who worship Him by choice.

God can do anything and everything better than we can. Jesus modeled the absolute perfection of the Father in everything He did. My attempts to mimic are genuine and sincere, yet incomplete. And yet He welcomes us into service where our continual lack is made up for, much like when Jesus multiplied the loaves and fishes. His additional touch to our best efforts elevates our impact to a level referred to by Jesus with confidence, *"and greater works than these shall you do"* (see John 14:12). Such an astonishing promise did not signify our greatness as much as it illustrates how His grace is the sufficiency that makes up for all that is lacking. That is not to imply that we don't mature and become better at all He's called us to be and do. It simply means the infinite greatness of God will never be equaled by us. His grace will be needed throughout eternity as we continually grow to be more like Him. Perhaps this is what is meant by Paul when he said, *"so that in the ages to come He might show the surpassing riches of His grace in kindness toward us in Christ Jesus"* (Eph. 2:7). This wonderful grace of God will be discovered, enjoyed, and depended upon for all eternity—*the ages to come.*

God is a covenant-making God, who delights in all that He has made for its intended purpose. If God were ever to have limitations of any kind, they would be self-imposed.

THE WILL OF GOD

My absolute favorite definition of the will of God found in Scripture is in the prayer that Jesus taught His disciples to pray: *"Your kingdom come, your will be done, on earth as it is in heaven"* (Matt. 6:10). That is the will of God—that the reality of His rule would be realized over every part of our lives and every aspect of life on planet Earth. Most everything I can think of that falls into the category of God's will for my life can be found in the answer to that prayer. *"On earth as it is in heaven."*

Bob Mumford gives us much-needed clarity on the subject of the will of God in his book, *The King and You:*

> We need to understand that there are two different words used in the Greek for our English word will, as it is used throughout Scripture. One is *boulema,* and the other is *thelema. Boulema* means the eternal counsels of God which are unfolding through the ages—His purpose—His determination. It is going to be done whether you and I like it or

not. God's intention will come to pass. However, *thelema,* which means God's wish or desire, most often depends upon the response of each individual for fulfillment.[2]

This was a very helpful truth for me to understand the will of God more clearly. The word *thelema* doesn't nullify that God is the absolute sovereign One. What it does do is reveal how the sovereign One wrote us into His design. This sovereign Lord chose us to be co-laborers with Him in the unfolding of His purposes. That means He works in and through His sons and daughters to implement His will in the earth. Let's face it, He can do everything He's called us to do significantly better than all of us combined. He can preach better, feed the hungry better, heal the sick and raise the dead better, and on and on. The point isn't that we question His ability. It's that we recognize our response-*ability.* Here is a perfect example of the usage of *thelema* in Scripture translated as "desires."

> *This is good and acceptable in the sight of God our Savior, who **desires** all men to be saved and to come to the knowledge of the truth* (1 Timothy 2:3-4).

What is God's will in this verse? It is that all men will be saved. Are all being saved? No. We have a part in seeing His desire accomplished in the earth.

He has given mankind the priceless gift of a will. That includes those who would surrender to Jesus as Lord and what those converted ones do with their assignment before God. In other words, if we send no one to share the Gospel with a particular people group, there will most likely be few conversions, if any. Was that God's will? No. He said, "Go!"

HIS RESPONSE TO OUR ACTIONS

Once again, God can do anything and everything better than we can. But He has chosen a partnership between Himself and redeemed humanity. A favorite verse in this regard is found in Acts 4.

> *And now, Lord, take note of their threats, and grant that Your bond-servants may speak Your word with all confidence, while You extend Your hand to heal, and signs and wonders take place through the name of Your holy servant Jesus* (Acts 4:29-30).

Here Peter prays for boldness so that as they declare God's word in bold confidence, God will respond by extending His hand to heal in honor of the name of Jesus they carry. They declared. God healed. Teamwork.

LEARNING FROM THE OLD TESTAMENT PRIESTS

My whole reason for starting this chapter this way is to affirm and yet challenge one of the great historic statements regarding revival: *Revival is a sovereign move of God.* Is that true? Absolutely. We could never experience a great move of God simply because we willed it to be so. Great moves of God are initiated by Him. No question. But my challenge to this idea comes in the notion that God willed the outpouring to end. The devastating result of this way of thinking is that we then assume that great moves of God are not to become a way of life, but instead are seasonal invasions of God to give us a booster shot to strengthen us for the next season. Consider this alarming thought: In the Old Testament, God lit the fire on the altar. But it was the priests who kept it burning. Why did the fire start? Because of God. Why did it end? Because of man. Any fire will die out if it runs out of materials to burn.

In the Old Testament, God lit the fire on the altar. But it was the priests who kept it burning. If the fires of revival end, man had something to do with it.

Proverbs warns, *"For lack of wood the fire goes out"* (Prov. 26:20) and describes *"fire that never says, 'Enough'"* (Prov. 30:16). It's rather simple, but fires burn as long as there is fuel to burn. If the fires of revival end, man had something to do with it. If my assumptions are true, then God has a way of life planned for us that is far beyond what most of us have experienced in this life. I like to think of it as a revival lifestyle. Others call it the ascended life, which is living from Heaven toward earth in unbroken fellowship with the Holy Spirit. Regardless of the title we give it, there is more. And it has been put upon us to pursue.

I don't consider this concept of God lighting the fire on the altar and man causing it to end to be in violation of the sovereignty of God at all. The will of God was revealed in revival. It is made possible by God initiating His will among us. His will is much like a stream that passes by us continuously. Dipping into that stream is my response to His will. He destined us for revival. I cooperated by yielding to His will by dipping into the stream.

My concern has little to do with anyone agreeing with me on the subject of sovereignty. My concern is that we will miss the heart of God for His people, for He is much more extravagant in His will for us than we have an imagination to capture. The bottom line is that many wait for Him to act. And oftentimes it is He who is waiting for us. We must learn to respond to what He's given us with acts of faith.

DOES GOD END A REVIVAL?

Even though this may seem to be a contradiction to my previous statement, God does, in fact, will for revivals to end. But it's not because He doesn't want us to experience an increase in the outpouring of His Spirit. It's because of what we've done with what He gave us. He once brought confusion to those building the tower of Babel because they could accomplish things outside of His purpose for humanity. That capacity to build was what He enabled them to do. As strange as it may seem, we have not always done well with great moves of God. Competition, self-promotion, careless lifestyles and efforts to control the move of God have all developed in times of revival. Did God want the revival to end? No. But He refused to add His presence to the *tower* that the leaders were building, allowing their own selfish interests to bring confusion to the builders.

Once again, throughout history we see times where God willed for a movement to end. But what's interesting is the why. He refused to add His blessing to the carnality and control of people. So yes, it was God's will for it to end. He did not want for His blessing to enable His people to distort or pervert His purposes on the earth.

HE DISCIPLINES HIS OWN

One of the most underrated realities in our lives is the discipline of the Lord. It's so valuable that it in essence validates the conversion of an individual.

> *But if you are without discipline, of which all have become partakers, then you are illegitimate children and not sons* (Hebrews 12:8).

It's not for punishment. His discipline comes to keep us from what kills and destroys and draws us into what gives life and freedom. Discipline is the entrance of more life. Proverbs, the great book on wisdom, states over and over again the wonderful value of this experience. I suppose the reason most of us don't like it is because our pride and self-interests die in the journey. But what we were designed to become is enhanced. Such is the life of God's disciple.

The result of this process is quite remarkable, especially when we consider the options.

> *For it is time for judgment to begin with the household of God* (1 Peter 4:17).

If God's judgments begin with us, we are transformed. When we are transformed, we are much more capable of representing the Lord well. This in turn results in people coming to Christ. On the other hand, if the judgment of God starts with the unbeliever, the only possible outcome is condemnation. They have no mediator, which for us is Christ Jesus. His judgments must begin with us. And there's no greater purifying element than the fires of revival.

IS FIRE GOOD OR BAD?

Fire has an interesting influence on people's lives in Scripture. The most obvious is the purifying factor. One could easily look to the refiner's fire in the process of purifying gold as a beautiful example. I am told that the one in charge of purifying this metal will place the container of gold over the fire until the impurities come to the surface as it melts. He carefully skims off the impurities in efforts to have the purest and most refined gold possible. He knows when it's completely pure: It's when he can look on the surface and see the undistorted image of his own face, much like in a mirror. It is this same process by which Jesus refines us. He does so until He can see His likeness in us. That is the real reason for refinement—to reveal Jesus on earth.

But it is important that we don't stop there, as so many have. The Bible says more of this transformational element. Fire has another purpose and effect, one I admit I don't understand, but enjoy very much. It was the tongues of fire that not only purified the 120 in the upper room on the day of Pentecost, but ultimately brought them great strength and encouragement. *"One who speaks in an unknown tongue edifies himself"* (1 Cor. 14:4). Only God would take the *fire* used to refine us and make it the tool that brings us encouragement and strength.

This reminds me of the dual effects of the Sword of the Spirit, which is the Word of God. It is a double-edged sword that has two very different results: It cuts, and it heals what it cuts.

For the word of God is living and active and sharper than any two-edged sword, and piercing as far as the division of soul and spirit, of both joints and marrow, and able to judge the thoughts and intentions of the heart (Hebrews 4:12).

The Word of God cuts deeper than our insight could ever take us. It goes into the unknown territory called *the heart of man*. Without God's light shining on our thoughts, intentions, and motives, we could never know the condition of our own hearts. But He doesn't leave us cut, open, and exposed. He brings healing to every area of our lives that we surrender to Him in times of exposure.

> *He sent His word and healed them,*
> *And delivered them from their destructions* (Psalm 107:20).

In the same way that the Word of God has two effects, the fire of God does as well. It both purifies and encourages. This is the mysterious yet wonderful grace of God at work.

FIRE ON THE ALTAR

We can see that in the Old Testament God lit the fire on the altar, and it was the priests who kept it burning. We also acknowledge that under the New Covenant every believer is a priest unto the Lord. So then, how do the priests of this hour keep a fire burning? What are the materials that are to be laid on the altar to burn? None of the following expressions are used to somehow control and motivate God to do what we want. All of them are things we can put on the altar to step more fully into what He has already designed and willed for us to experience.

— The Public Confession of Sin —

This has often been used by God as the catalyst to igniting revival fires, which is the mighty outpourings of the Spirit. God responds to repentance and humility. Throughout revival history, Christian college campuses are especially known for this manifestation. God loves and honors the humility expressed in these times, often releasing greater and greater measures of the *rain from Heaven.* This is a very legitimate attractant to, and fruit of, revival. But sometimes the problem comes when that alone becomes our definition of a revival. Then you actually need more sin for revival to continue. We must find out how revival can be expanded and sustained as a result of the confessed sin. It must go somewhere.

Humbling ourselves before our brothers and sisters often draws the blessing of God upon our gatherings. Whether it is in confessing our sins, or serving one another through honor, or simply preferring one another in a ministry situation, it's all valuable and celebrated by God. Humility and revival go hand in hand.

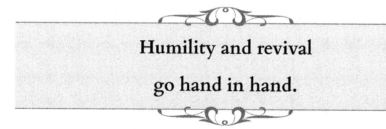

Humility and revival go hand in hand.

— Traditions and Practices —

Throughout history these elements have often hindered the move of God. Traditions are not necessarily evil. In fact, some of them beautifully illustrate the grace of God in a previous time or upon a previous generation. There is much to learn from the rich traditions of the Church. I enjoy attending the gatherings of our traditional brothers and sisters, as I learn how we got to where we are. It can be a wonderful celebration of

God's sovereign influence on our past. It also reinforces thankfulness for those who paid the price to bring us to where we are today.

Most of our families have traditions that we value and practice around Christmas and Thanksgiving, and/or other times of the year. Our family has a song that we sing at our holiday meals. It's called, "Father, we thank thee." I remember hearing it year after year when I was a small child. And now my grandchildren are being exposed to the same simple, yet powerful tradition.

There are also traditions that are essentially evil. They were designed by people who were resistant to the move of God. Some of the time it's not the tradition that is the problem; it's the mindset that accompanies the tradition. We've all heard it said, "We've never done it that way before," which is in direct conflict with the heart of God, who has promised to do *a new thing* among us. Those two values are in opposition to one another. Surrendering to the purposes of God is always the need of the moment, regardless of the cost.

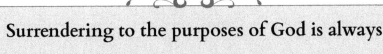

Surrendering to the purposes of God is always the need of the moment, regardless of the cost.

You might say that if God wills for there to be a revival, no one can stand in its way. And in principle, I agree. But in practice, not completely. Let me explain. First of all, I've seen God pour out His Spirit on people who were not hungry and were not seeking Him. There's no question that these encounters were sovereign visitations of God. Perhaps Saul's encounter with Jesus on the Damascus Road would qualify as a great example. We can't afford to ever forget that God can do whatever He wants, with or without our cooperation. But most of the time He works in line with our yielded participation. He's the one who says if we seek Him, we will find Him. Yet here's a rather sobering passage on what God thinks of the power behind some of our traditions.

> *"Neglecting the commandment of God,* **you hold to the tra-dition of men.***" He was also saying to them, "You are experts at setting aside the commandment of God in order to keep your tradition. "For Moses said, 'Honor your father and your mother'; and, 'He who speaks evil of father or mother, is to be put to death'; but you say, 'If a man says to his father or his mother, whatever I have that would help you is Corban (that is to say, given to God),' you no longer permit him to do anything for his father or his mother; thus* **invalidating the word of God by your tradition** *which you have handed down; and you do many things such as that"* (Mark 7:8-13).

This is a frightening warning. Jesus starts by saying that what God has commanded is *neglected*, while the traditions of man are *held* onto dearly. This word *neglect* means "to dismiss or release." In a legal sense it means "to divorce." The picture Jesus offers here is that people remove themselves from any covenantal responsibility to carry out God's commands. The word *hold* is primarily "an exercise of power." Religious leaders use their authority to empower the inferior traditions of man over the Word of God. The other word worth taking note of in this passage is *invalidating*. Traditions can invalidate God's Word, which means "to render void, deprive of force and authority." One translation says "to render power-less." It sounds blasphemous to say that a tradition of man can deprive

God's Word of authority or power. In reality, nothing will ever remove the authority of His Word. It's not that traditions are more powerful. I believe Jesus is talking about the effect of traditions on the human heart. Sometimes traditions disengage a person so completely from the power released in God's Word that the all-powerful Word becomes powerless to them. There is little to no impact in their lives from the transformational power released in that Word.

Here, Jesus is addressing a deliberate choice where the values and edicts of man are treasured more than the Word and will of God. There are countless stories of revival where someone had to lay down a tradition, often good ones, in order to see more of what God intended to do. Perhaps that's the picture given to us of Peter and the Lord's command to eat what was unclean and forbidden by Jewish law. He had to lay down a belief (tradition) in order to be a part of the mighty outpouring among the Gentiles. (See Acts 10.) *"While Peter was still speaking these words, the Holy Spirit fell upon all those who were listening to the message"* (Acts 10:44).

Sometimes those traditions are actual truths taken beyond their intentional impact or original design. For example, one of the most helpful phrases I heard many years ago was that *the Kingdom of God is now, but not yet*. That helped me so much as I was learning to seek first His Kingdom as commanded, but needed help to understand why it wasn't all being manifested here and now. But today, most every time I hear that phrase it's to tell me that I can't have what was promised by God in the Scriptures. Another way to put it is that the *not yet* has become the hiding place for unbelief. Unbelief is always the outcome of improper traditions. And they exist in the place that the demonstration of truth is supposed to occupy.

The unhealthy dependence on traditions must be laid on the altar for revival to advance, for nothing, no matter how noble it appears, can take the place of the Holy Spirit's direction over the human heart. There is nothing greater than the presence of God. And He chooses to manifest upon His people. It is that manifested presence that distinguishes the people of God from all the other people of the earth. (See Exodus 33:16.)

It is that manifested presence that distinguishes the people of God from all the other people of the earth.

— Impure Motives and Intentions —

These issues of the heart must be dealt with to see the great moves of God. Sometimes confessing such things, sometimes simply laying them down before the Lord attracts that fire from Heaven. Both the Word of God and the Spirit of God expose impure things in us. It always surprises me how long I can live with an attitude He doesn't approve of and not know it. But when God points it out, it must be dealt with quickly and thoroughly.

I am reminded of Moses, who failed to carry out a command of the Lord to circumcise his sons. This has to be one of the most unusual stories of a great man of God who at one point failed the Lord. God actually sought to kill Moses because of this. We don't know the behind-the-scenes story, but can assume that Moses broke a serious command of the Lord over his life.

— Reconciliation —

There's quite an emotional and mental distance between the 12 disciples of Jesus, who thought they were better than each other, to the point that each argued their case, to the crowd of 120, which included 11 of the original 12, who gathered in one accord, apparently without offense.

— Personal Goals, Dreams, and Ambitions —

Sometimes the hardest things to lay on the altar are the things that we came up with from the principles of Scripture. It's even harder to lay down the things promised us by God. Abraham did so and entered into a whole new level of relationship with God. Moses threw down his rod, which turned into a snake, and was then required to pick it up by the tail. Picking a snake up by the tail is how you get bitten. But when God says to do it that way, it's the only way you don't get bitten. This process keeps us dependent upon God. Obedience puts us into the grace where God keeps the snake from biting.

— Associations —

As strange as it may seem, in order to experience more, we sometimes have to leave our associations with people who oppose the move of God.

— Rights —

"Why not rather be wronged?" (1 Cor. 6:7). This unique laying down of personal rights, for the sake of the whole, is sometimes the offering needed to attract the fire of God.

— Abilities —

Yielding the purpose of our skills/gifts, surrendering what we know how to do can be the most challenging part of this journey. It's not that we are necessarily selfish in this endeavor. It's that self-confidence can interfere with God confidence or faith.

— Reputations —

Protecting personal dignity and appearance to others is often what must be put on the altar for revival to continue. Many a fire has gone out because people were unwilling to do something that offended the masses. It's not that we are to be careless or brash and call it obedience or a life of faith. And yet the sad reality is that many are more willing to offend God by not obeying His commands that require risk and boldness than they are to offend people by living in a way that stirs up controversy. We call it many things, like being a good witness, not bringing shame to the name of the Lord, and preserving our God-given reputation. But most of the time I think it's the fear of man. That single element has caused so many to stop short of God's intent and purpose for their lives. We either fear God or fear man. We can't do both at the same time. One has to go.

We either fear God or fear man.

We can't do both at the same time.

— Acts of Faith —

Faith always offends the stationary. Our cooperation with Him to do His will is often the most difficult offering to give Him. It would seem that it wouldn't be so, but we actually have entire schools of thought built around avoiding this one thing. And what's worse, avoiding the will of God is considered a virtuous part of many believers' theology. It's hard to imagine that 2000 years ago our leaders could have anticipated such a departure from the commandments of Jesus. And then to make it worse, it would be considered maturity or virtue. Healing and deliverance are expressions of this one thing called *salvation, (sozo)*—"salvation, healing and deliverance— spirit, soul, and body." Salvation was always to touch the whole man. Luther and Calvin, who were great leaders of the Reformation, reacted to the Catholic notion that the existence of miracles confirmed their theology was right. But these great reformers threw the baby out with the bath water, so to speak. They denied the need for miracles as a normal expression of our faith, thus creating the idea that it is noble to believe without signs and wonders. And while that has definite value, it has created a powerless Gospel that is applauded as virtuous. The reality is, miracles lead people to Jesus, which in turn strengthens our resolve to follow and believe. The failure of the nine lepers to return and give thanks to Jesus for healing them of leprosy was not a commentary on the legitimacy of the miracle. God is never judged by the response, or lack thereof, of people. He is revealed in His work, which in this story was the healing of leprosy.

Once again: Healing is not the whole Gospel. But neither is the Gospel whole without it.

One of the great areas of offense in our day is that sometimes people who operate in the supernatural with miracles, signs, and wonders have bad character. It's extremely frustrating for me, as I emphasize purity in character equally with my emphasis on power wherever I have influence.

Tragically, I find that people are quick to judge the person of questionable character as automatically being a false prophet, or something similar, while never learning how God views the situation. I would never claim that God simply overlooks sin in our lives because we perform miracles. And while a person being a false prophet is certainly the case at times, more often we are faced with something we don't really understand or know how to handle. It is this: God has a different value system than we do. When He releases the miracle of healing, let's say, through the life of a person of weak character, He is not validating the individual. He is validating His Word! He has chosen to allow His Word to work in the life of the believer or unbeliever. It might be wisdom for us to find out why God would do that, as there is a value in His Word revealed in this circumstance that not even many who claim to be *Word-centered* really understand.

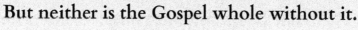

Healing is not the whole Gospel.

But neither is the Gospel whole without it.

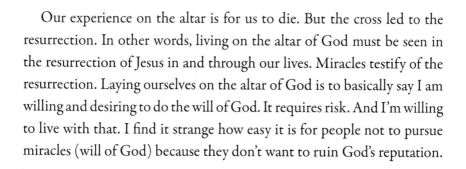

Our experience on the altar is for us to die. But the cross led to the resurrection. In other words, living on the altar of God must be seen in the resurrection of Jesus in and through our lives. Miracles testify of the resurrection. Laying ourselves on the altar of God is to basically say I am willing and desiring to do the will of God. It requires risk. And I'm willing to live with that. I find it strange how easy it is for people not to pursue miracles (will of God) because they don't want to ruin God's reputation.

Without resurrection power in and through our lives, there's not a reputation to ruin. Our own fear of looking bad to others often hides behind the notion, "I might bring a bad reputation to the Gospel."

In essence, the way we keep a fire burning is to put ourselves on the altar in whatever way seems fitting in that moment. From confession of sin, all the way to being willing to look bad (take risk) for the move of God to gain traction in the hearts and minds of people.

HEAVEN IS THE MODEL

It basically comes down to this: Revival continues, not by giving attention to revival, but by giving our complete attention and affection to God Himself. The corresponding obedience is Christ-centered. The question is not, *What can I get from God?* but, *What else can I give Him?*

Revival continues, not by giving attention to revival, but by giving our complete attention and affection to God Himself.

Heaven is presence-centered in every way. Everything that exists in that reality is directly connected to God's presence. In a very real sense, He is the reality of Heaven, as there is nothing there that is apart from Him. The Kingdom of God is the expression of Heaven in the here and now, which is the reality of His rule over people's lives and human affairs.

This leads us to the nature and essence of revival. It is the manifest presence of God having an effect on all we are and do. His fiery presence rests upon all who live before God with this kind of *yes*.

NOTES

1. Simeon Walcher Harkey, *The Church's Best State or Constant Revivals of Religion* (Miami: HardPress, 2017).

2. Bob Mumford, *The King and You* (Old Tappan, NJ: Spire Books, a div. of Fleming H. Revell Company, 1974), 27.

Chapter Nine

THE HINDRANCE
OF MATURITY

*A true revival means nothing less than a revolution,
casting out the spirit of worldliness and selfishness, and
making God and His love triumph in the heart and life.*
—ANDREW MURRY

WHAT you know can keep you from what you need to know if you don't remain a novice. Learning is vital. But equally important is the ongoing flexibility to learn more as a child would.

The walk of the believer is one of continual conflict. And oftentimes, that conflict is in our own minds as we grapple with the teachings of Scripture that appear to be in contradiction. They aren't in contradiction, but it certainly can appear that way to the casual observer. For example, we know that in the Kingdom of God, giving leads to receiving. We also know that going low in humility is how one is to be exalted or promoted. And while we may struggle with the application of these truths, we know enough to get ourselves started. But let me introduce what might be the hardest of all Kingdom conflicts: We must grow into maturity by becoming as a child.

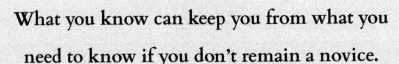

What you know can keep you from what you need to know if you don't remain a novice.

Most of the time maturity in the Church is anything but being child-like. It is usually seen in the austere life of a seasoned saint, who has for the most part overcome the basic temptations of life and is a great example of Christ in character. And what could be wrong with that, you may ask. Nothing, actually. Illustrating character is of paramount importance. And yet the ability to enter the reality of God's dominion on earth, in the here and now, is determined in part by my willingness to become as a child.

> *But when Jesus saw this, He was indignant and said to them, "Permit the children to come to Me; do not hinder them; for the kingdom of God belongs to such as these. Truly I say to you, **whoever does not receive the kingdom of God like a child will not enter it at all**"* (Mark 10:14-15).

When Jesus spoke of the Kingdom, it was often related to a miracle that was about to happen or already had. That is because the Kingdom of God is in power, not words. (See First Corinthians 4:20.) Many people think it's virtuous to choose character over power. Jesus never gave us the liberty to choose between the two. That is a man-made option.

On the other hand, I am saddened and frustrated by many who have chosen power over character. It is never okay to condone those whose personal lives are a wreck, and yet they pursue the miracles of God, which they often use to justify their immoral lifestyle. That is an absolute lie from the enemy himself. It is tragic that any believer could fall for such devastating deception. And yet is it any more ethical to pursue character without power? Look at it this way, what is more valuable—not to grieve the Holy Spirit or not to quench the Holy Spirit? Of course, we consider both to be of equal value. We grieve Him through impurity in thought, intentions, and actions. The command not to grieve Him is focused on character. But to quench the Holy Spirit has more to do with stopping the flow of something. It is power-centered. Character and power are the two legs we stand on. Having one longer than the other will have serious impact on the overall health of the body.

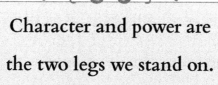

Character and power are
the two legs we stand on.

Choosing character above power is certainly more popular and socially acceptable. But since when did it become possible to develop the depth of character Jesus intended for us apart from obeying Him? And is it not a commandment of the Lord to heal, deliver, and cleanse? (See Matthew 10:8.) Did He ever suggest that His commission into a miracle lifestyle was optional? Is it possible that the one part of our character that rarely gets developed in those who pursue character separately from power is childlikeness? I'd like to suggest that the challenge of pursuing character over power has given place to the death of childlikeness in the nature of the Church. Being as a child is no longer considered maturity. And in such an atmosphere, maturity has become a hinderance to advancement in the Kingdom, which ultimately is a hinderance to revival. Maturity, as it is commonly portrayed, is a hinderance to revival.

In a power-filled miracle lifestyle, childlikeness must be developed and embraced. In the move of the Holy Spirit, we rarely know what we're doing. We follow His lead in the dance. Dependency is the ongoing theme for the child. Their parents or caregivers supply food, clothing, shelter, encouragement, instruction, inspiration, opportunities and so much more. They are sustained, at least in a healthy home environment, through the supply of others. Welcome to childlikeness. Maturity often wars against these values, in the name of becoming established in the faith.

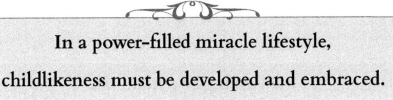

In a power-filled miracle lifestyle, childlikeness must be developed and embraced.

In the Mark 10 story mentioned above, the disciples had an adults-are-more-important-than-children value system. It is the most common idea even today. Consider this, Jesus taught that we can only enter what we've received. And we must receive His realities through a childlike heart. There's another very similar insight given to us from the teaching of Jesus in the Sermon on the Mount.

> *Blessed are the poor in spirit, for theirs is the kingdom of heaven* (Matthew 5:3).

The way to receive the Kingdom is to become as a child, and the way to possess or advance in the Kingdom is through being poor in spirit. Remember, the Kingdom, as taught and illustrated by Jesus, is most often the here and now reality of His dominion. Perhaps we could say that childlikeness and being poor in spirit are two sides of the same coin. They are very similar in nature and purpose.

Being poor in spirit is not thinking little of ourselves or being depressed in any way. Childlikeness is not being foolish or careless. Both virtues (being poor in spirit and childlikeness) are seen in our being flexible, teachable, adventurous, simple in our approach to life, and able to laugh a lot. In that frame of mind, the smallest experiences in life are worth celebrating. It's not just the cancer healed, or the promotion at work, or the degree you worked so hard to earn. It's also the random phone call from a friend. It's the unusually good meal or the delight of watching children or grandchildren playing and enjoying life. I love watching parents enjoy their children, whether it's at a playground or in an airport terminal. It is pure joy and delight. It is life.

The qualities of being poor in spirit and childlikeness are both fed by joy. And both are recognized in being carefree. Being carefree is different from carelessness.

RESPONSIBILITY OR CONTROL

Some historians credit the end of revivals to the control exhibited by the leaders. I don't know that any genuine leader in a revival would sit down one day and decide to take control of what God is doing. That would be rather dumb. But in our efforts to be responsible leaders, we often fail in this area.

Knowledge promotes control. Back to our opening statement: *What you know can keep you from what you need to know if you don't remain a novice.* Learning is not the problem. Rather, the problem is that in learning we tend to overestimate how much we know of what is knowable. Even in that, the learning is not the issue. The pride and independence created when we become self-assured trip us up.

ARMCHAIR QUARTERBACKS

We all have opinions about most everything in life. Opinions are easy to form. Just a little bit of information, with the right set of circumstances, and an opinion is birthed. They are not necessarily bad or evil. It's just that it's hard to learn wisdom from an opinion because it has no consequences. Decisions, on the other hand, are great places to learn wisdom if one so desires.

If I have the opinion that touching a hot stove won't hurt, but never touch it, I can live a lifetime convinced I'm right. But touching the stove enables me to learn, quickly.

I love sports and have enjoyed watching my favorite team play on TV. For me, American football is perfect for the television medium. A play generally takes a few seconds, and then there's a break. Announcers are able to use the time to inform the audience of the play, what's at stake or even the backstory of a particular player. It's easy for me to stay engaged. But I, like most every other fan, have opinions on which player should play the most, what kind of plays they should call, and on and on. Whenever they run with the ball and they lose yardage, I have heard myself saying, "Why didn't they pass? Can't the coach see the defense is always ready to stop that play? They had a widereceiver in the open!" And when they pass, and it doesn't work, I wonder why they didn't run with the ball. The point is, it's easy to have an opinion on the game when it costs me nothing. But the players, coaches, and owners all pay for their decisions.

If a wrong play is called, it's wisdom to learn from it. But the armchair quarterback is always right and lives with the subtle deception that he knows what he's talking about. If calling or playing a game in any sport was that easy, there would be no professional level, as everyone would be able to do it. We watch because we like to watch the excellence formed through devotion/discipline and skill/athleticism.

One of the areas where there are the most armchair quarterbacks is in the Church. When people don't have to pay for their opinions, it's easy to have one. As leaders, we often receive letters, emails, and counsel from people who have never done anything of significance with their lives.

The carelessness in this arena is not just around church life. I remember several years ago, one of our pastoral staff members had prostate cancer. He received a lot of advice about medical treatments he should have, and/or the health care directions he should take. One of the most stinging things said to him was that he brought this upon himself because his diet was wrong. What's amazing is this was spoken to him by someone who had never shared a meal with him and knew nothing about his diet. Yet they were confident in their perspective, as they no doubt had read an article somewhere that helped them form an opinion. For them, the information age informed them into greater ignorance. Learning without experience is theory. Only the wise know the difference between the maturity that comes from experience and the maturity that comes from theory. Revival critics illustrate this truth better than most.

REVIVAL CRITICS

The restaurant critics of church life have rarely cooked a meal, so to speak. They quickly discredit something they didn't pay a price to obtain.

It's like critiquing a painting by a child. The easiest statement in the world for the art critic is to state, "It's no Rembrandt!" But is it supposed to be, in order to be of value? Much of what is criticized or opposed is such a painting. It's not what it could be, but neither is the artist finished with their development.

I remember going to Argentina with Randy Clark in 1997, I think. I wanted to go simply because Randy invited me, and it would be a great time to learn. And I did. But I also wanted to go because I had heard what God was doing there, and I wanted to participate and learn from their example in revival. It was such an extraordinary time for me, for reasons beyond what I can mention.

While I never mentioned this to anyone, I wanted to see if what we were experiencing was anything similar to what they had been walking in for years. Here was my conclusion: The move of God for these leaders was like a ripe, red apple. It was sweet to the taste and very enjoyable. And while they would never say they had "arrived" they were further down the road than we were. But what I also learned is that what we were experiencing was like a young apple, just starting to grow on the tree. While it was not fully formed or fully mature, it was still 100% apple. It was still 100% revival.

I remember a couple of years after that trip, I was a speaker in a conference with one of the primary leaders of their revival. We had some private time together at a meal, which was the ultimate privilege for me. We talked for quite a long time through his translator. When I told him what we were experiencing, he said, "This is revival! Not everyone agrees with me, but this is revival!" He just affirmed that our *apple* was truly an apple, even though it was still developing. What encouragement this was to me, from a true father of revival. And may that apple continue to grow and become all that God intended.

DO WE GROW UP OR GROW DOWN?

In the Kingdom, maturity is in part measured by becoming like a child. This is not to promote or approve of childish behavior. But it is to clarify what real maturity looks like to God. It's simple.

Perhaps you've heard someone say, "The more I learn, the more I know I don't know." My late brother-in-law, Jim Grubbs, used to tell me that. He was a highly trained college professor, who absolutely loved learning. He read two to three books a week, for the 40-plus years I knew him. I remember early on hearing him tell me that in all his learning, he was most aware of what he didn't know. That kind of learning is maturity, in a biblical sense. It is wisdom. We are supposed to mature and pursue wisdom, understanding, and knowledge. These things are vital to our lives. But with true learning comes humility. I'm reminded of King David and his approach to life in this regard:

> *But I am poor and needy;*
> *Yet the Lord thinks upon me.*
> *You are my help and my deliverer;*
> *Do not delay, O my God* (Psalm 40:17 NKJV).

There's good reason to believe that David was the richest man on earth during the time of his reign. We see the lavish spending on the temple of the Lord during Solomon's reign but often forget the materials were paid for and set aside by David. Yet his approach to life was, "But I am poor and needy." I don't think this statement was for show. It made it into the canon of Scripture. Neither do I think this was his struggle with self-esteem. It was honest. When we see ourselves as we are, we will never think too highly of ourselves. Being filled with self-criticism is not the answer, either. His poverty was discovered in approaching God, as He is our all-in-all.

It could easily sound like I'm resistant to bringing caution or seeking counsel. I'm not. But I'm not interested in counsel from someone who simply has an opinion. And while I am responsible to recognize the word of the Lord, sometimes from someone I wouldn't have intentionally sought out for counsel, I am more likely to listen to a person with experience.

REVIVALS AND THE IGNORANT

Glorifying ignorance, or the lack of insight, is an improper goal. It's certainly not one I hope to accomplish. In one sense, this chapter is mislabeled in that maturity is never a hindrance. My issue is that what we often call "maturity" is our greatest hindrance.

My emphasis is not to keep us from pursuing the knowledge of God, as it is a biblical mandate to seek Him. One of the strong promises of Scripture declares this concerning the effects of the gifts of Christ upon the Church; they will bring us to the *unity of faith, and the knowledge of the Son of God.* (See Ephesians 4:12-13.) The pursuit of wisdom is a mandate!

Historically, God moves most often on those who don't know what they're doing. It's not that God prefers the ignorant. It's just that the ignorant are more flexible and more likely to trust Him beyond their understanding. He is able to do more through people who realize what they don't know. The ignorant, as it pertains to the moves of God, are the best tools, as they bring fewer biases into the movement.

Our challenge is to remain childlike in the midst of a great outpouring that promises to take us into greater places of influence in culture.

It's not that we don't learn, or increase in our insights and convictions. That is automatic and necessary. But for the same reason God often uses the ignorant for His greatest moves, so He looks for us to remain dependent, regardless of how much we've learned. We never mature beyond trust and dependency on God. And those who do, disqualify themselves from much of what God intended to do in their lives. The stronger the qualities of trust and dependency on God are in a person's life, the more mature they are from Heaven's perspective. Consequently, the more He is able to do through them.

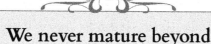

We never mature beyond
trust and dependency on God.

One of the more interesting responses to revival came from many of the leaders from the Church in England who visited Wales to see what God was doing. They gave glowing reports, acknowledging that it was truly from God. But some of them consciously left the revival because they knew they would impact it in an unhealthy way. They recognized that in this case, the revival needed to be led by the young, who had to trust. That is a stunning conclusion. They weren't afraid of influencing toward evil, as they were truly living holy lives and only wanted for the people of God to live fully surrendered to Jesus. They simply realized the principle that I'm trying to address here: What you know can keep you from what you need to know if you don't remain childlike.

THE WARNING OF JESUS

Jesus gave us a warning concerning wheat and tares that seems to be applicable in the context of revival as much as in any other area I can think of in the Christian life.

> *"Sir, did you not sow good seed in your field? How then does it have tares?" He said to them, "An enemy has done this." The servants said to him, "Do you want us then to go and gather them up?" But he said, "No, lest while you gather up the tares you also uproot the wheat with them. Let both grow together until the harvest, and at the time of harvest I will say to the reapers, 'First gather together the tares and bind them in bundles to burn them, but gather the wheat into my barn'"* (Matthew 13:27-30 NKJV).

Everything God does in us is good. Obviously. It always carries His likeness and blessing. But the enemy works, too, especially during times of revival. I don't for a moment want to glorify the devil, but neither do I want to be ignorant of his devices. He is the angel of light, who seeks to deceive. So, he planted tares in this story. Tares look just like wheat until the wheat matures. The weight of the grain of wheat causes it to bow as it becomes mature. This illustrates in a wonderful way what real maturity looks like: We bow before Him with greater humility and trust.

I understand that the Jews have called tares "illegitimate wheat." If you remember the clarification of Scripture on being legitimate sons and daughters of God, you'll remember that being disciplined by God is the evidence.

*If you endure chastening, God deals with you as with sons;
for what son is there whom a father does not chasten? But if
you are without chastening, of which all have become partak-
ers, then you are illegitimate and not sons* (Hebrews 12:7-8
NKJV).

Correction done correctly, and received correctly, builds humility and
trust. I remember my own children, when I had to bring discipline into
their lives, wanted to sit in my lap that evening. They naturally drew near,
as they knew that my correction was not rejection or punishment for my
sake. It was for theirs. So, the correction of the Lord endears us to Him as
the loving Father who always looks for our best.

But back to the story of wheat and tares: The warning is that in our zeal
to have only wheat (only the works of God among us) *we will* unintentionally destroy what God was doing. He didn't give further instruction
on how to recognize the difference. He said, "Don't touch it."

I am not saying that we are not to give oversight to a move of God.
I'm just saying that in our zeal we will destroy what God is doing, because
what He is doing is not always recognizable through our lens of experience and insight. Once again, we come back to the place of humility and
trust—the real sign of maturity.

Chapter Ten

TRANSLATING REVIVAL

The Christian conscience permeated society after this
Great Revival as yeast does dough. Education was
Bible-oriented again. Teachings about witchcraft were
removed from textbooks. Believers, as in prior years,
began caring for the elderly in their homes, and an
intense sympathy was created for the poor. Genuine
national prosperity followed. It was called
The Industrial Revolution.
—MARY STEWART RELFE, PhD[1]

I N her wonderful book, *Cure of All Ills,* from which the above quote was
taken, Mary Stewart Relfe, PhD, addressed what revival looked like under
the leadership of Jonathan Edwards. She said that Edwards concluded:

...a full-fledged revival will involve a balance between
personal concern for individuals and social concerns.
He assessed that religious meetings, prayer, singing, and
religious talk will not promote or sustain Revival in the
absence of works of love and mercy, which will "bring the
God of love down from heaven to earth."[2]

Revival is Heaven come to earth, in the most beautiful and practical way. I love Edwards' perspective so much. Longevity in a great move of God happens when we take what we've experienced in our corporate gatherings and translate them into practical expressions that bring improvement to our communities. Translating revival into God's intended outcomes satisfies the cry of our hearts to know God through personal encounter while overflowing into the privilege to make Him known, for He is the perfect Father who longs for the hearts of people to be open to His transformational love. This is the drive within the heart of every true believer: for the masses to be touched by the love and power of God and brought into His Kingdom through salvation.

Revival is Heaven come to earth, in the most beautiful and practical way.

I've been in meetings where the presence of God was simply overwhelming. People were overcome by God. Sometimes their encounters went on for hours and hours, and sometimes for days. The easiest thing to do whenever we see something happen that is not in our experience, or even the history of whatever spiritual tribe we're from, is to reject or judge it as error. I find it a most disgusting type of arrogance for me to judge the experience of another person by my own experience, or worse yet, by my own lack of experience. The latter is the most common error, for sure. The attitude of many is that *God would never do that to another*

person, unless He's first done that for me. While most of us would never say it like that, that is the approach I've encountered most.

FRUIT OF REVIVAL

The revivalists of old knew enough not to judge the manifestation immediately. They waited long enough to see fruit. When someone comes out of a profound encounter, and they love Jesus more, and/or have a greater hunger to read God's Word, and/or are more deeply in love with their spouse, it's God. (The devil is not known for that kind of fruit. He comes to kill, steal, and destroy. So, wherever we see death, loss, and destruction, we know the devil has been there.) In such encounters, the simplest person, with no outstanding gifts, becomes a world changer. My book, *Defining Moments* is all about this phenomenon. People become world changers in that God sends them into the most dangerous or challenging environment, armed only with the love of Jesus, and there's dramatic impact. If only more people knew what was available by seeking Him wholeheartedly, it would change everything. And I do mean everything: in us, for us, and through us.

I remember an interesting experience we had with a young boy, about eight years old. He was touched powerfully by God. His mother called me later that night to express her concern. Her son lost the ability to talk. Of course, I understood her anxiety and listened to her describing him in that moment. But she went on to say that every time she mentioned the name Jesus, he would weep. God marked that young boy for Himself in this encounter. His speech returned the next day. But that family will never forget God's unique way of calling their child to Himself.

Resisting the idea of being overwhelmed by God is more of a trust issue, exposing our need to be in control, than it is a fear of deception. He warned us of this issue:

> *So I say to you, ask, and it will be given to you; seek, and you will find; knock, and it will be opened to you. For everyone who asks, receives; and he who seeks, finds; and to him who knocks, it will be opened. Now suppose one of you fathers is asked by his son for a fish; he will not give him a snake instead of a fish, will he? Or if he is asked for an egg, he will not give him a scorpion, will he? If you then, being evil, know how to give good gifts to your children, **how much more will your heavenly Father give the Holy Spirit to those who ask Him?*** (Luke 11:9-13).

Whom are we seeking? What are we asking for? Is it not *more of Him at any cost?* At this point, many fear deception more than they are concerned with lack (going without the blessing that God has reserved for them). If we are seeking Him, asking for Him, we do not need to fear being deceived. In fact, many embrace deception by fearing it. It really is an issue of mistrust.

Our being in control is what got us into most of our problems. You'd think we'd learn. And at this point someone is quick to point out that self-control is a fruit of the Spirit, which is absolutely correct. But think about it. What is a fruit of the Holy Spirit? It's where the Holy Spirit has control in our lives, to produce a fruit worthy of the nature of Jesus. I have self-control when I'm under the Holy Spirit's control. And when He is present in power, things happen that are outside of my understanding. Translating revival means I have to have something to translate—even if it surpasses my understanding.

I have self-control when I'm under the Holy Spirit's control.

KEEPING FOCUS

The revival fires must continue to burn, our encounters with Jesus must continue and increase, and our impact must grow. But learning how to *translate revival* from what happens in the meeting to our influence outside of the room is absolutely critical for sustaining the outpouring. Jonathan Edwards understood this and helped to usher in what historians call The Great Awakening. A revival, stewarded well, will always increase and impact the world. I believe we are at the beginning stages of the Third Great Awakening.

A revival, stewarded well, will always increase and impact the world.

Whenever we make revival about ourselves—our experiences, our personal ministries expanding, our churches growing, increasing our position in societal influence, and a whole host of other *fruits of revival*—we lose the capacity to sustain the move of God. Seeking first the King and His Kingdom is the context in which all the rest is added. But when I pursue *what He intends to add,* I level off in my maturity, and therefore limit the measure of Kingdom I can manage as a good steward.

For example, Beni and I have an orchard of about 30 fruit trees. We don't grow apples by trying to grow apples. We grow apples by attending to the health of the apple tree. The tree provides the fruit if we take care of the tree. The growing ministries, great numbers of conversions, and greater influence in society are the apple. It's all fruit of something else. As long as we make sure the tree (seeking God's face) is the priority, bearing supernatural fruit that glorifies Him is normal and natural.

MANIFESTATIONS IN REVIVAL

By now you should know that I am no longer afraid of outward manifestations that often happen when the Holy Spirit comes upon someone in power. I've seen the results in people's lives. It is astonishing to see the change that God can do in moments that we as pastors have tried to do with those same individuals for years. That is absolutely true.

Instead of being surprised when extreme things happen when the Spirit of God comes upon them, we should be surprised when they don't. When someone as powerful as the Almighty God touches you, the surprise should be that you're still alive. And while that will appear to be an extreme overstatement to many, it really is the truth. We are frail human beings, in the hands of a powerful but compassionate Father.

The physical manifestation is never the goal any more than getting wet should be the goal of water baptism. There is a profound transformation of one's life in water baptism: buried with Christ in His death, and raised with Christ in His resurrection. It is real. Outward manifestations in revival must represent something much deeper than *shaking and weeping*. When it's genuine, God is always working beyond the obvious. At Gate Beautiful, the lame man walked, leaped, and praised God. He was physically healed. But he was also emotionally and spiritually healed. God works deeply.

For what it's worth, these manifestations have been seen in most every revival in recorded history and from every known denomination. And while there have been efforts on the part of denominational historians to remove the manifestations from the record, due to the embarrassment they cause, they are still in the original manuscripts.

God adds a price to every revival, one that will cost us in associations, friends, and position before the world. Most of the time the cost has something to do with our personal dignity—the concern over what people think of us. I believe this to be an expression of the fear of man. Revival provides us with the sobering reminder that I can live in the fear of God or the fear of man, but not both. And it is revival that forces such a decision.

Revival provides us with the sobering reminder that I can live in the fear of God or the fear of man, but not both.

Our dear friend, Heidi Baker, of Iris Ministries International, had one of the most extreme encounters I've ever heard of. Let's just say, it lasted for days. But without that, she has stated that she never would have had the courage to endure the persecution, beatings, and imprisonment. And then you add the heartbreak of the opposition from other believers. She can never doubt what God did. But then, a life of ease doesn't need that kind of courage. And those who oppose generally don't see the need for extremes because the goal is life without conflict. Perhaps it's time to put ourselves at risk enough to increase our need of the God who invades people's lives with more of Himself.

HOW DO WE TRANSLATE THAT?

I love, and mean absolutely love, seeing the power of God touch people's lives. I can't imagine ever feeling different about it, as His glorious presence becomes so pronounced that we become discipled by the glory. It is truly beyond description. And I have seen a few occasions where such a glory/power is seen in a public place. We have great stories of miracle services breaking out in a grocery store and revival-type encounters being released at a theme park. I am not opposed to that and have told our people to call me when the Spirit of God falls in Costco. My concern is not an embarrassment for what God might do in public. It's for the fact that such a power encounter, in our own lives, was to produce something for God's glory. And the thing that testifies of His greatness in the public setting is not my shaking. It's the fact that the fear of man has been shaken out of my life, and now I can take a stand whereas before I would cower in fear before those I work with.

One of the greatest threats to the move of God happens when we define revival in too restricted and confining terms. Forgive the oversimplification, but, for example, for many people revival is weeping, or laughing, or falling and shaking. And when that represents our definition of a move of God, our goal is that we'll see people fall under the power of God in the Real Estate Office or the grocery story, or wherever. We have to remember that our message is not revival. Neither is it manifestations, or experiences or spiritual gifts. It is Jesus. And He can be known, encountered, and trusted fully with our lives. That is our message.

Translating revival must enhance this message of Jesus, the Savior who can be known, encountered, and trusted with our lives. And it needs to be seen where it matters most: our average, everyday life. While I love the thought of seeing God's glory fill a restaurant, my cry is to see the manager of the restaurant, who was touched powerfully by God last week, now take a stand among his fellow workers. That is really where we see the ever-increasing glory of God realized in a more permanent way. It's among those who represent Him well in purity, power, and compassion. The courageous stand taken by this manager is a stand that he would have found difficult only two weeks before. What happened? The power of God came upon him in his weekly small group meeting, and now he's different. Everyone, including his wife and children, can see it. He is the embodiment of courage. The fear of man was broken off of his life. And it seemed to happen in a moment. God now says "amen" to his words and actions, making them powerful. And as long as he doesn't invite that monster back into his life, he will illustrate the kind of boldness that can only be found in Christ. I love the Proverbs 28:1 statement on boldness: *"The wicked flee when no one is pursuing, but the righteous are bold as a lion."* If ever we needed people who model this kind of boldness, it's now. And there's no better way than to be apprehended by the Lion of the Tribe of Judah. His courage becomes our courage. It's not philosophical in nature. It is in our possession through the divine encounter. His nature becomes expressed through us in the experience.

I love the thought of the glory of God filling our homes to the extent that even the neighbors notice something unusual happening with us. But I also want the purity, love, and compassion to benefit the neighbors. And for the single mom, who was profoundly touched by God last month, I look for her to be able to take a stand against the harassment of her ex. Instead of her being manipulated for sexual favors and the like, I want to see the power of God upon her for a bold witness of the Gospel of Jesus Christ. Both she and her ex need a display of the Holy Spirit kind of courage that can only happen when He is present.

I want to see the businessman or woman who is accustomed to taking bribes or compromising the truth take their rightful place as a righteous representation of God's Kingdom. Or the pastor who is governed by a board of carnal leaders take their stand for the complete and absolute abandonment of all for the purpose of seeking the face of God, regardless of what it looks like. Revivals must be translated into something that will benefit the average citizen, so they can *"taste and see that the Lord is good."* (See Psalm 34:8.) Notice the words, *taste and see*. *Taste* is our experience. *See* is our perception. What we experience will always shape our perception. The world around us is crying out for the authentic display of a God who loves them. It is time that they experience God through the lives of those apprehended for revival, that their perception of Him is radically changed. This is the fruit of revival. As God touches us in dramatic ways, so He can use us beyond ourselves, to feed a hungry world.

KILLING THE FEAR OF MAN

I don't believe there has ever been a person who God used in profound ways that did not have to deal with the fear of man. One of the things I've been learning is that if I don't live from the praises of men, I won't die by their criticisms. It is absolutely true. This, of course, doesn't give us permission to be rude or careless. It just means we're willing to make decisions for God that cause us to lose favor with people. If you can't do that, you can't live in revival.

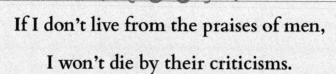

If I don't live from the praises of men, I won't die by their criticisms.

Most of us who have studied revival have favorites. It's not that some were necessarily better than others. We just tend to admire the ones who remind us of our own journeys.

In conversation, we might say to one another, "Oh, John Wesley. What a great man!" or "That George Whitfield was such a powerful preacher of the Gospel." My own family was powerfully impacted by Smith Wigglesworth, Maria Woodworth-Etter and Amie Semple McPherson. I love their stories. Especially the ones that help me to see they were normal people. None of us feel qualified to be a superstar. But God in us makes nothing impossible.

Each of us, according to our Christian backgrounds, have the names of our heroes put to memory. And rightfully so. Most of you reading this book will recognize the name Charles Finney if for no other reason than I have spoken of him several times in this book. Yet do you recognize the name, John Nevin? He lived at the same time as Finney and was as well-known. But he was an opponent of the revivals of Finney. If there's no other lesson to be learned, it's that history does not treat the critics of revival well. Their names are forgotten. And every revivalist you can mention had opponents of equal and sometimes greater position in the eyes of man. They had to endure such opposition to step more fully into all that God had ordained for them.

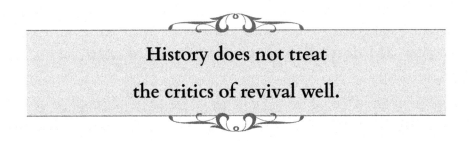

History does not treat

the critics of revival well.

PROTECT THE HOUSE

It is vital that we learn how to protect what God is doing in our churches, small groups, and homes. We never have to apologize for or explain God. He can defend Himself quite well. But we also must learn that what goes out of the house must be that which is beneficial for society and affects culture for the glory of God. This is translating revival.

NOTES

1. Mary Stewart Relfe, PhD, *Cure of All Ills* (Montgomery, AL: The League of Prayer, 1988), 23.

2. Jonathan Edwards, *A Treatise Concerning Religious Affections* as quoted in Stewart Relfe, Ph.D, *Cure of All Ills*.

Chapter Eleven

WHAT IS REVIVAL "UNTO"?

A state of constant revival is both possible and
practical, and every Christian ought constantly to aim
at it, and labor and pray for it . . . May God in great
mercy send us constant, ever continuing, all conquering
revival . . . May the work commence and never cease
until millennial glory shall beam upon us, and the
triumphant anthem roll over the whole earth: "The
kingdoms of this world, have become the kingdoms of
the Lord and His Christ! Amen."
—SIMEON W. HARKEY[1]

THIS quote from the 1800s is especially dear to my heart, as the author, Simeon W. Harkey, is one of the few people I've ever heard declare *revival should be the norm.* I like to put it this way: Revival is the normal Christian life.

Earlier in this book, I addressed the importance of staying true to the foundation, which in the Christian experience is the day of Pentecost. What happened there must remain in place. We can add to it, build upon it, and experiment around it, but we must stay true to what got us here, the foundation. The reason is that God is always taking us to a greater glory. He is always taking us somewhere deeper, more intimate, and more glorious; and it will always have a greater impact on humanity. I personally think the target is always *the glory of God filling the earth.*

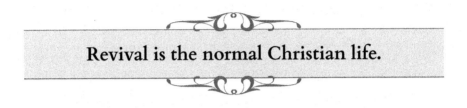

Revival is the normal Christian life.

PENTECOST IS REVIVAL

Pentecost is an invasion of His glory, permeating His people, overflowing with the effect of righteousness and justice in the earth.

Pentecost is the outpouring of the Holy Spirit where the people of God are being launched into things we do not understand, cannot explain, and dare not control. This amazing day in history is an honest revival: one without the agendas. The sooner we come into the realization that we are all prone to create agendas, the better. For then we can pursue His purposes, knowing we have a limp, a weakness, a bias. And by His grace, and His grace alone, that weakness can be covered by His overwhelming presence so we can enter fully into what He has for us in this life; it is always beyond what we would have imagined or asked for.

Pentecost creates momentum to build for the glory of God. It may include organizations and buildings. But honestly, we can do that without revival. What's more important is the building of ideas, values, relational structures, and creative expressions that all work to illustrate the nature of God and model His purpose for humanity on earth. This is a measurable way to see the impact of Heaven on all we are and do.

THE WISDOM OF RECOGNIZING WEAKNESS

Isn't that the reason for Jesus teaching us to pray, *"lead us not into temptation"*? The Bible already tells us that it is impossible for God to tempt us because He cannot be tempted with evil. So why ask Him not to tempt us? Because it forces us, no matter how great our successes, no matter how great His purposes over our lives, to live aware of our constant need of His grace.

I am reminded of this concept in the warning recorded in Proverbs, addressing the person of excellence. It says they will stand before kings. But then it says if we recognize that we have an appetite for what the king has (possessions, pleasures, position), we should put a knife to our own throat to hold that desire in check. Otherwise, we will be driven by appetite and not purpose and will ultimately compromise our position to serve and influence the king. (See Proverbs 22:29–23:2.) In the story of revival with bias and an agenda, it is wisdom to recognize our own appetites that could compromise what God is longing to bring into our lives.

This isn't to say that our agendas are evil. Most of us pursuing revival can give chapter and verse for our biases. They are based on what we have learned or experienced in our journey with God. In some cases, our convictions come from what we've heard from the stories of revival in history. Hold to those values and convictions tightly! But don't allow them to determine what you are willing to learn in the future. In most cases they are wonderful insights—until they interfere with what God intends to do next.

THE POWER OF JOY

For example, when I think revival looks like tears, my preaching and ministry will be looking for that manifestation to affirm we are now in revival. And yet I've seen times when God had a different plan. He brought joy. And what made matters more complicated, the people who least deserved it are the ones who received it the most. The revival experts (critics) had a heyday with that one. "These people should be weeping before God in repentance! They've been complacent sinners for years. Joy is not the appropriate response. This is not revival!" And yet many of these joy-filled people were changed into passionate followers of Jesus in the experience. They became better spouses, parents, and workers. Isn't that the kind of fruit we long to see from those who repent?

One of the more interesting stories in the Bible in this regard is found in Nehemiah 8. This is where we have the great statement, *"the joy of the Lord is our strength."* But what precedes that outcome is often forgotten or ignored. They read the Word of God in the public square. People stood for hours, listening to the Word and heard what God required. They began to weep as a result of seeing how far away they were from God's standard for their lives. The priests ran among the people and told them to stop!

> *Then Nehemiah, who was the governor, and Ezra the priest and scribe, and the Levites who taught the people said to all the people, "This day is holy to the Lord your God; do not mourn or weep." For all the people were weeping when they heard the words of the law* (Nehemiah 8:9).

Sometimes joy is a greater manifestation of faith than weeping. I can always hang my head and weep, realizing how unworthy I am on my own.

To truly rejoice in Him means I have to look above my issues, and look to His accomplishments on my behalf.

From what I've seen in Christendom, a weeping crowd is the evangelist's dream. That's where we invite people to the altar to repent. That is an appropriate response, and it absolutely has its place—unless it's not what God is doing. In Nehemiah 8, the people of God were instructed to have a feast and celebrate, because they understood the words of the law. They didn't celebrate because they had fulfilled God's requirement for their lives. It was because they saw truth and understood it. I wonder how many more victories we would experience if we simply rejoiced our way into the victory just because we heard God's voice, saw His heart, and said yes to His commands.

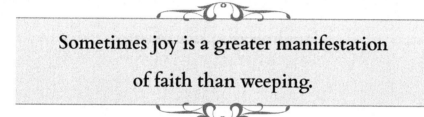

Sometimes joy is a greater manifestation of faith than weeping.

Both the Nehemiah story, and the situations I've seen in recent church life, sound a lot like grace. People who don't deserve it are given joy. Grace is underserved favor, which seems to perfectly describe this situation. This is the standard of Scripture, *"It's His kindness that leads to repentance."* (See Romans 2:4.) A hard lesson for me to learn in this regard was that what tears are to repentance, laughter is to salvation.

I think a person could be born again for only a week and still have a bent on how they seek God for revival. It doesn't take us long to form biases. This is where we must mature in relation to our pursuit of more of God: revival! We too often reduce our discernment for the move of God down to specific acceptable manifestations and not the discernment of His actual presence. It's hard to recognize Him in a public setting if I don't develop those *skills* in private. In my personal interaction with Him is where I learn to recognize Him when He steps into the room. And please don't be offended by my phrase, *when He steps into the room.* I know He is already with us. But living unaware of Him makes it difficult to recognize when He shows up in an increased manner or in a different way with a specific agenda. Jesus lived aware of Him and became an example for us:

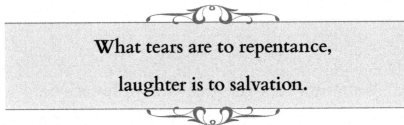

> **What tears are to repentance,**
>
> **laughter is to salvation.**

> *One day He was teaching; and there were some Pharisees and teachers of the law sitting there, who had come from every village of Galilee and Judea and from Jerusalem; **and the power of the Lord was present for Him to perform healing*** (Luke 5:17).

The Holy Spirit, the power of Heaven, already rested upon Jesus. The fact that Jesus recognized that the power of the Lord was present to heal implies He could be there for another reason: deliverance, preaching, correction, prophetic encouragement, etc. Jesus, seeing what the Father was doing, cooperated with that power to perform the miracles that revealed the Father's heart to people. It should be upon each of us to learn to recognize Him and then learn to recognize His heart. For only then can we know what He just walked into the room to do. I sincerely believe that this by itself enables us to go deeper into the move of God than if we insist on holding to our biases. If we do that, we will typically only experience what we have faith for and not what He plans to do. Recognizing what He is doing is a critical component to discovering what revival is to lead *unto*.

BEING CO-MISSIONED

There are several commissions of Jesus in the Gospels. The most famous, of course, found in Matthew 28, is what we call the Great Commission, rightfully named because it reveals the heart of God for placing us on planet Earth.

> *And Jesus came up and spoke to them, saying, "All authority has been given to Me in heaven and on earth. Go therefore and make disciples of all the nations, baptizing them in the name of the Father and the Son and the Holy Spirit, teaching them to observe all that I commanded you; and lo, I am with you always, even to the end of the age"* (Matthew 28:18-20).

Similar passages in Mark and Luke each add to the overall picture of this commission:

Mark's version:

> *Go into all the world and preach the gospel to all creation. He who has believed and has been baptized shall be saved; but*

he who has disbelieved shall be condemned. These signs will accompany those who have believed: in My name they will cast out demons, they will speak with new tongues; they will pick up serpents, and if they drink any deadly poison, it will not hurt them; they will lay hands on the sick, and they will recover (Mark 16:15-18).

Luke's version:

Thus it is written, that the Christ would suffer and rise again from the dead the third day, and that repentance for forgiveness of sins would be proclaimed in His name to all the nations, beginning from Jerusalem. You are witnesses of these things. And behold, I am sending forth the promise of My Father upon you; but you are to stay in the city until you are clothed with power from on high (Luke 24:46-49).

We know that while each of these decrees varies in tone and information, they are not in conflict. Instead, they complement each other. All three provide us with a unique glimpse, with a more complete picture of our assignment. It's not my intent to fully study these passages here and now. But I would like to address two specific things addressed here that can help us with the question, *what is revival unto?*

First of all, being commissioned implies empowerment for a specific purpose. In this case, it is to follow the footsteps of the One who commissioned us and carry on His work. In light of this, one of the focuses is on making disciples *of* nations. The next is to make disciples *within* nations. This is a significant distinction that has profound ramifications on how we live, think, pray, and act.

Before you balk at the idea of discipling nations, remember God calls us, the Church, a holy nation; only a nation can disciple a nation. But only a united nation can have that kind of influence and clout on actual nations of the world. Because revival is life in the glory, and His glory unites, we can see how discipling nations can and must be possible—by living in the glory.

And the second part is what we're more accustomed to: make disciples within nations. We do both of these by walking in the footsteps of the resurrected One, who has a solution for every personal issue, as well as every international issue. Nations were His idea. And He has a plan.

Combining these two focuses in the commission reminds us to *stop for the one,* as Heidi Baker has declared it, and serve them for their personal transformation. But the second part is to inspire us that we would never lose sight of the responsibility to bring about cultural change in society itself through the Gospel of the Kingdom, thus, discipling nations.

That Gospel is the good news of living under His rule/dominion. It affects and redefines all of life. This *as-it-is-in-Heaven* reality is to be just that—a revelation of the Heaven to come through the examination of the believer's life in these realms: spirit, soul, and body. Jesus' ministry impacted each of these three areas, and that was before the cross and resurrection. How much more is to be seen, now that the believer is the eternal dwelling place of the Holy Spirit.

THE GOAL OF TRAINING

Making disciples, not converts, is our mandate. The beautiful ambition of all training in the Kingdom of God is for us to become like Jesus in all we are and do. Jesus has intentions for us that are far greater than any of us would think possible. This is the standard of Scripture: *"but everyone, after he has been fully trained, will be like his teacher"* (Luke 6:40). Likeness is the goal.

Jesus has intentions for us that are far greater than any of us would think possible.

Jesus modeled the best discipleship program the world has ever seen. He trained His original 12 disciples through word, example, and empowered opportunities. Those opportunities were the times Jesus commanded and enabled them to do the same as He did. They returned from those missionary-type journeys with the stories of the miracles and deliverances they were involved in. The following four areas addressed in His training provide a skeletal example of His relational journey with 12 men that we call discipleship:

— Character/purity —

His teaching, which included correction, focused on issues of ambitions, thinking, and behavior. They were to live in a manner consistent with the example that Jesus set for them in managing their inner world.

— Love/compassion —

Jesus was constantly moved with compassion for people and their needs. Such compassion was followed with a supernatural solution. Much of His training prepared the twelve to care for others. It started with how they viewed other disciples, but extended to the hungry crowds they were wanting to send home.

— Power/authority —

This was specifically aimed at healing and deliverance. It's interesting to note that power and authority didn't function on their own. In Jesus' example, we see both power and authority flowing through His compassion for those in need. Paul put it this way, *"faith works through love"* (see Galatians 5:6), to illustrate that these are always used in serving others effectively.

— Dream/significance —

This is probably the one on the list that many will have trouble with, as it appears to have little to do with revival. Let's look at it this way: If revival is supposed to be "unto" something, it has to be as a result of transformation, and not more meetings (which I love.) Jesus addressed this issue four times in John 14,15, and 16, whereby His disciples were given a promise from God that only Solomon before had been given; they could have whatever they asked for. So here the friends of God have been given a blank check. Will we spend it building our empires? Or will we ask for nations?

The effect of succeeding here is a reformation where society itself is transformed from the inside/out. Transformation will affect the laws that society creates. But it's important to note that the laws are not what brings transformation; it's the Holy Spirit working in and through His followers to demonstrate the reality of Heaven on earth.

Authentic transformation starts with the mind. Paul instructed us in this way: *"be transformed by the renewing of your mind"* (Rom. 12:2). A transformed mind transforms a person. And a transformed person can transform a city.

Transformation is the ambition of Heaven. It can be measured in healthy families; productive lives that contribute to the overall health of our communities; prosperity of soul that affects the overall health of body, mind, and emotions; ever-increasing hope for all that God has purposed for our lives on earth; as well as ongoing financial increase that comes because of divine purpose. From there, cities take on a unique design, contributing to an overall expression of the creative nature of God on the earth. My hope is that we will see a Reformation combined with a Renaissance to more fully reveal the nature and covenant of God in the healing of the land.

Revival reveals the holiness and power of God.

Reformation reveals the heart and mind of God.

Renaissance reveals the beauty and wonder of God.

These will be discussed more thoroughly in a later chapter.

LET'S PAINT A PICTURE

As I wrap up this chapter, let me paint a picture that should help us in seeing the effect revival is supposed to have in the shaping of culture itself.

First, picture a brick wall in your mind. And for illustration's sake, let's say that that wall is made up of 30 rows of bricks, each row upon another until it reaches the desired height. That wall represents society, with all its unique placement of gifts and assignments from God. Each layer represents a different segment of society. While God loves all of us the same, not all have the same favor. Jesus spoke of the person with five talents (measure of money), another with two, and yet another with one (see

Matt. 25:14-30). The wonderful truth that applies to all, regardless of how we start, is all have unlimited potential through faithful use of what God has given us. A good reminder is that Jesus had 12 disciples, but only three of them were allowed to participate in some of His endeavors. God sovereignly selects people for different roles. Struggling with that issue must be dealt with in life, or we will respond with jealousy for the one with more or feelings of superiority over the one with less. Either posture is dangerous.

Back to the wall: The bottom rows are the poorest of the poor, and the top rows represent those who have been placed in a high place of influence. This is either through their positions of rule, like a politician or a CEO of a corporation, or through fame, like an actor, an actress, or a professional athlete. The top row is made up of the people with position that shape and create culture.

Now imagine the fire of revival hitting that wall. Revival always starts at the bottom with the poor and burns upward. And while it may not always mean the economically poor, it is always the poor in spirit. As the revival is stewarded well, it spreads to other layers of bricks on the wall. When a revival has been stewarded well long enough, it eventually begins to shape the values, ambitions, and behaviors of those who shape culture. These are the mind molders, constituting the top layers of bricks on the wall. Most of the time these positions are abused and used for personal gain and self-promotion. But that was not the purpose for their gift, any more than Jesus gave the treasury box to Judas so he could steal. Everything God gives us has a divine purpose and is intended to bring Him glory. And everything He gives us can be used in the direct opposite reason for which God gave it. The point is, when revival has its full effect on society, touching the upper layers of this illustration, touching those who appear to be untouchable, culture changes. Fire burns upward. Transformation flows downward.

POWER AND WISDOM

Power ignites the beginnings of revival, but wisdom sustains it. The failure to apply the standards of Scripture, revealing the mind of Christ to the everyday affairs of life, is what will starve a revival in the same way a fire dies without fuel.

Power ignites the beginnings of revival, but wisdom sustains it.

I believe that cultural transformation is what ignites or launches us into a reformation. Culture is basically the way people live and approach life. It includes things like relational boundaries, identity, values, ambitions, purpose, hopes and dreams, and a whole host of other effects of God's direct influence over all we have and are. The process of going from cultural transformation to reformation involves learning how to live in wisdom, which positions us to reign in life. The cultural transformation that leads to reformation is the result, at least in part, of the gift of God called wisdom, which is the mind of Christ.

Just to whet your appetite: Geneva still lives under the influence of a reformation that happened 500 years ago. Rolex, Cartier, the United Nations, the YMCA, the World Bank, and a whole host of other entities exist where Calvin and others believed God's ways were best and that He had answers to every dilemma we could experience in our world. These values and truth created an incubator effect in a part of the world where excellence, creativity, and possibility become normal expressions of life. Because of the profound impact of a reformation on the generations, I'd like to declare, *we owe our children, our grandchildren, for many generations, a reformation.* The proper stewardship of revival as a seed, will set us up to taste and see why we're alive. Revival is unto reformation.

NOTES

1. Simeon W. Harkey, *The Church's Best State or Constant Revivals of Religion* (Sydney: Wentworth Press, 2019), 103.

Chapter Twelve

THE COMING PENTECOST, COMING GLORY

Revivalists are born in the tension between glory
to glory. Yes, there is a glory in a former season or
expression of outpouring; however, as wonderful as that
is, there is more. There is increase. God is greater than
the last season of awakening and a period of revival.
Could it be that we have not seen a consistent, sustained
revival because we are expecting God to continue things
as is, when in fact, He deliberately and intentionally
wants to turn up the heat?[1]

PENTECOST is a historic event that declares God's intent for the future. He doesn't go backwards. Neither does He try to restore us to the good ol' days, in the sense that there is nothing new. We have the great challenge to maintain what is valuable to God, which includes our God-given history, while at the same time position ourselves for the increase and change He intends to bring. Taking up that challenge is glorious beyond our imagination or desire.

Understanding what happened at Pentecost, beyond the obvious, will help us to see the need for this ongoing work in us for all time. Pentecost was glorious for reasons above and beyond common understanding. To see this one event as a pattern for all time is necessary and profitable. But to see it clearly, one needs to examine the root system of this experience. For that, we must go back to Genesis to examine the first time the *house of God* is mentioned in Scriptures. It is an unusual moment, but filled with so much hope and promise.

THE ROOT OF GENESIS

It stands to reason that because God sees the end from the beginning, and He is truly sovereign over all, that He would plant the seeds of His ultimate intentions in the Book of Genesis. And He did. In fact, there are so many things initiated in the book of beginnings that to miss them is costly, as they pertain to divine purpose. A personal favorite that has great impact on the Great Commission through Jesus is found in chapter one. *"God blessed them; and God said to them, 'Be fruitful and multiply, and fill the earth, and subdue it'"* (Gen. 1:28). He made the earth for mankind, but the heavens for Himself. (See Psalm 115:16.) His plan was for those made in His image to be His delegated authority over the world as we know it. In this way God rules, but does so through us. This picture continues after the Fall of Man through sin. Jesus restored us to a place of purity and purpose, giving us power and authority to preach good news to *all creation*. (See Mark 16:15.)

The second major truth pertaining to our identity and purpose is found in the first mention of *house of God* in the whole Bible. We know that the theme *house of God* is huge in Scripture, gaining momentum and design in the New Covenant.

The Church is not buildings or organizations. The Church is people—living stones, being built together into the house of God, in order to house a spiritual priesthood. This identity was declared in Exodus 19:6 and in Isaiah 61:6. Both times the Lord said it would happen, speaking of a future date and time. But here, Peter declares it is now! It was coming. But it now is.

> *And coming to Him as to a living stone which has been rejected by men, but is choice and precious in the sight of God, you also, as living stones, are being built up as **a spiritual house for a holy priesthood,** to offer up spiritual sacrifices acceptable to God through Jesus Christ . . . But **you are** a chosen race, **a royal priesthood,** a holy nation, a people for God's own possession, so that you may proclaim the excellencies of Him who has called you out of darkness into His marvelous light* (1 Peter 2:4-9).

Of the many *houses of God* in the Old Testament, only two were prophetic illustrations of the New Testament Church. One is called the Tabernacle of David. Priests ministered to the Lord 24/7 in worship and intercession. This type of ministry is modeled so well through Mike Bickle and the IHOP ministry. David's tabernacle is spoken of as a last-days ministry in Amos 9:11-12 and reaffirmed as New Testament reality in Acts 15:15-17. But the second illustration, found in Genesis 28, is the one we need for this chapter.

> *Then Jacob departed from Beersheba and went toward Haran . . . He had a dream, and behold, a ladder was set on the earth with its top reaching to heaven; and behold, the angels of God were ascending and descending on it . . . Then Jacob awoke*

*from his sleep and said, "Surely the Lord is in this place, and I did not know it." He was afraid and said, "How awesome is this place! **This is** none other than **the house of God,** and this is **the gate of heaven"** (Genesis 28:10-17).*

Theologians commonly agree that whenever we find the first mention of a subject in Scripture, it sets a standard for the rest of the Bible to affirm or add definition to, but never to undermine. This principle is fascinating as it pertains to the subject of God's house, as there is no building mentioned at all, nor is there even a group of believers gathered, as we would see in Acts or the Epistles. What we do have is a man with a dream—and a God encounter—in the open air. And that is called the "house of God." Apparently, wherever God dwells, that is His house.

There is one qualifying statement in Jacob's response that could be quite perplexing. In his experience, he called the house of God *the gate of Heaven.* As mysterious as this may sound at first, it is actually quite wonderful and reasonable when we consider who God made us to be.

A gate is a place of transition between two realities. For example, I have a gate that takes us from my driveway to my backyard and vice versa. I also have one that takes us from our backyard into our organic garden and back again. The point is that the gate is what gives access to either place from the other.

Believers are seated in Christ, in heavenly places. (See Ephesians 2:6.) That is our eternal home, which we enjoy in measure now. And yet we are citizens of this world as well. Here we see our unique position of dual citizenship.

The picture that Jacob alluded to was a house that was a gate on the edge of two realities: Heaven and earth. That has never been more real, or even possible, than in New Testament times when the Church finds her place in Christ, *"far above all rule and authority and power and dominion, and every name that is named, not only in this age but also in the one to come"* (Eph. 1:21). This should lead to a perception of Pentecost that should cause us to ache for it once again.

This view of Pentecost is to give us a perception of how God has chosen to do things in this world. First let me say, God is God; He is sovereign over all and can do anything, any way He wants. Whenever He chooses to work in a certain way, it is not because He is limited or restricted. It is because He is love. And love works with wisdom for the sake of all that He has made.

If we pray for the sick, and they are healed, what has just happened? Health is a reality of Heaven, which is His world. No sickness can dwell there, as it is a place where His perfect and complete rule is demonstrated. Our faith and/or obedience brought us into agreement with His will, revealed in His nature (see Exod. 15:26), and in our purpose and call (see Matt. 10:8). Healing, the reality of His world, came through the *gate* into this world. Is that not, at least in part, what He meant when He told us to pray, *"on earth as it is in heaven"*? (See Matthew 6:9.) The house of God is a gate.

PENTECOST AND THE GATE

One hundred and twenty people gathered in true unity and prayed. We don't know the schedule of this prayer gathering, if it was 24 hours a day, 7 days a week for 10 days, or if was for several hours a day or what. We do know they prayed until He came.

When the day of Pentecost had come, they were all together in one place. And suddenly there came from heaven a noise like a violent rushing wind, and it filled the whole house where they were sitting. And there appeared to them tongues as of fire distributing themselves, and they rested on each one of them. And they were all filled with the Holy Spirit and began to speak with other tongues, as the Spirit was giving them utterance (Acts 2:1-4).

Tongues is a wonderful gift from God and is used for edification. The only gift to be used for our own benefit. But in this context, I don't want to make our subject to be tongues or any other manifestation. It is about Him coming upon us and filling us with Himself. That is the goal, that we might impact the world around us, in His name, as Jesus would if He were in our shoes.

Picture now with me the idea that the Church, the 120 believers, were the *gate between two worlds*. Is it possible that this visitation of God that is recorded here is a manifestation of heavenly realities upon these His people? Let me explain. It says a *noise* came from Heaven. That word for *noise* can be translated "roar." Then we read of a sound, like a violent wind entered the room. That word for *wind* is in the New Testament twice. In this verse it is "wind," and the other time it is translated "breath." Is it possible that what is recorded here, the roar of God's own breath, is what filled the room? The two manifestations of this marvelous grace released over them were seen through natural descriptions: wind and fire. I don't think it is a coincidence that the writer of Hebrews writes, *"and of the angels He says, 'Who makes his angels **winds**, and His ministers a flame of fire'"* (Heb 1:7). And again, He writes, *"Are they not all ministering spirits, sent out to render service for the sake of those who will inherit salvation?"* (Heb. 1:14). Angels enforce the purposes of God on His behalf in our lives. They also render service for those who are born again. While it is foolish to worship angels, it is equally foolish to ignore them. Jesus spoke of them and part of the role they would play with Him, who was the prototype of the believer, when He said, *"Truly, truly, I say to you, you will see the heavens opened and the angels of God ascending and descending on the Son of Man"* (John 1:51). While Jesus is the eternal Son of God, here He is called the Son of Man. For me that emphasizes the intention of God's world to cooperate with born-again people. Angelic activity is unseen by us, usually. And probably should be. But it is vital that we believe what the Word of God says, regardless of our experience. We are the place of angelic activity. We are a gate of Heaven.

While it is foolish to worship angels, it is equally foolish to ignore them.

WHAT WAS THE SOUND?

It appears to me that there were a great number of angels present on the day of Pentecost, as they had great effect on how the day was described: wind and fire. But the corresponding result is what moves me most. The roar of Heaven, the breath of God, released a sound over the city of Jerusalem.

> *And when this **sound** occurred, **the crowd came** together, and were bewildered because each one of them was hearing them speak in his own language* (Acts 2:6).

The story goes on to say that Peter preached the Gospel to the crowd that gathered and that 3,000 people were saved that same day. (See Acts 2:41.) This is astonishing, especially when you consider that the initial response of the people was to mock and reject the manifestation of God's presence upon His people. (See Acts 2:7-11.)

What I want to draw your attention to is the *sound* released through the 120 over the city. I think it's a bit foolish to think that in an international city of this kind, that people speaking in foreign languages would attract a crowd of multiplied thousands. Even in a city like Redding, which has been far from an international gathering place, that kind of gathering would never happen. If ten people stood on a street corner speaking in Spanish, or Lithuanian for that matter, it would never cause people to leave their homes and businesses to gather around a crowd of foreigners. Never. I'd like to suggest that the breath of God, released over the yielded hearts of 120 people, created a sound, much like the breath of a musician releases a sound as they breathe over the mouth piece of a saxophone. And that divine sound summoned people to their destiny, even though they first ran into an offense. Oftentimes, our destiny is on the other side of an offense. (If we can make it over that hurdle, we can step into all that God intended. Certainly, that is what happened to the Syrophoenician woman who wanted healing for her daughter. Jesus said He couldn't give the children's bread to dogs. She had a chance to get offended, quite easily, actually. But she didn't. And her daughter was healed.)

Oftentimes, our destiny is on the other side of an offense.

I find that God often exposes our bent toward offense whenever He starts to move in a supernatural fashion. It often looks like anything but divine. The question remains: How hungry are we?

It is so wonderful that the 120 people first prayed in unity. It may have been what brought them together. And then again, unity might be the result of their praying and repenting together for ten days. Regardless, that unity enabled them to endure the temptation to be offended at one another's experience or be controlled by the fear of man as they see the city's initial response to their encounter.

The end result is what we all long for: Three thousand souls came to Christ. But it didn't stop there. The process of addition to the Church was daily.

The picture I've tried to paint is how the Church is the gate of Heaven, strategically positioned between two worlds—Heaven and earth—and how even Pentecost happened consistently with that concept of partnership between two worlds through yielded delegated authority.

THE IMPACT OF PENTECOST

I think fewer people would be offended at the subject of Pentecost if they could just see the effect of that ongoing experience on the cities they loved and served. Sometimes the offensive things or the way people have misapplied certain truths or experiences have caused really good people to "throw the baby out with the bath water." So many standards are changed in this one day—the one day the Holy Spirit had complete control of.

"And it shall be in the last days," God says,
"That I will pour forth of My Spirit on all mankind;

and your sons and your daughters shall prophesy,
and your young men shall see visions,
and your old men shall dream dreams;
even on My bond slaves, both men and women,
I will in those days pour forth of My Spirit.
And they shall prophesy" (Acts 2:17-18).

The Church is often known by the barriers we create. And yet the outpouring of the Holy Spirit was to destroy barriers, revealing the heart of God for humanity. Look with me at the walls we have built that God destroyed in that one day. If for no other reason, we need another Pentecost to destroy the barricades we have built "in Jesus' name."

Every Race: He said He would pour out His Spirit upon *all* mankind. No race is better than another, nor is any race inferior. The arrogance that would give birth to such nonsense is obliterated in Pentecost. Only in the afterglow, when we've lost the original flame, do we find occasion to return to such inferior ways of thinking.

Male and Female: He said that both sons and daughters would prophesy. That responsibility to speak on God's behalf is not reserved for men only. That deception, which has been fueled by a horrible misunderstanding of Paul's teaching on women, is destroyed in Pentecost. In the Gospels, only men were counted in a crowd. At Pentecost, everyone was counted. The move of God creates a level playing field. Unfortunately, only in the aftermath of such an outpouring are the destructive standards of *men only* restored to church life.

Every Age Group: Young men see visions, and old men dream dreams. The point is, you can't be too young or too old. The value of every age only becomes clear in the anointing of Pentecost, where people are celebrated for who they are in God, without stumbling over who they are not. This is a vital thing for a time when culture worships youthfulness and ignores the benefit of age. It's the two together that gives a more complete picture of the nature and heart of God.

Every Social Class: He said, *"even on bond slaves."* Thankfully, slavery is no longer legal. And while there are places around the world where it still happens, it is recognized by most everyone as evil. So, this verse takes on even more special meaning, as the experience of Pentecost is also for those who would be slaves. In no way does this verse condone slavery. Instead, it asserts that not even slavery can create a barrier that keeps a person outside of the glorious, heavenly encounter with the Holy Spirit found in Pentecost. Even the slave becomes positioned to change the world!

Pentecost created a level playing field for every race, men and women alike, every age, and every social and economic class. It's time we return to the theology of Pentecost, as it's been so long since the fire of His presence burned up the nonsense we have since created in His name. The weeds have grown in the absence of His overwhelming presence. It's time to be overcome again.

Pentecost created a level playing field for every race, men and women alike, every age, and every social and economic class. It's time we return to the theology of Pentecost.

The beauty of church life, let alone city life, must be done by valuing the whole Body of Christ. This must include the third-wave/charismatic/Pentecostal branch, as well as the liturgical parts, and everything in between. We are much better together than we are apart. But it goes beyond our traditions and beliefs; it must include women restored to their place of honor, with every race celebrated for who they are, and every age and class honored from God's perspective. This enables us to value unique cultures from around the world, realizing that there are glimpses of who Jesus is that can only be seen by our embracing people outside of our religious comfort zones, which will in turn enrich all of our lives.

The baptism in the Holy Spirit was important enough that Jesus said they were not to leave Jerusalem without it. This experience is not to create those who have, versus those who have not. It is both a command and an invitation to be immersed in God beyond the point of fighting for human dignity, and yield completely to Him. It changes our perspective on everything. The hunger for revival must include this baptism as a primary focus, as this is what Jesus commanded them to pursue. Dr. Michael Brown quoted Oswald Chambers' thoughts on the baptism of the Holy Spirit:

> Looking back, Oswald Chambers could say, "The baptism of the Holy Ghost does not make you think of time or eternity; it is one amazing, glorious now."[2]

I love that so much. *One amazing, glorious now!* When the hunger for revival increases, there is much talk about dealing with sin and compromise. And it is for good reason. We must deal with these issues. But I have this sense that oftentimes people settle for inferior things because we have not clearly championed their purpose in life.

We keep women in check, criticize the youth, treat one race or culture with disregard or even disrespect. What happens when our theology allows for such conduct, in Jesus' name, of course? People lose interest, as they lose sight of why they're alive. And while we might have been able to keep a generation tethered to our standards of church disciplines in generations past, it's not likely today. God has no grandchildren. Everyone must be born again and live a life consistent with that experience. Jesus did not come to make bad people good. He came to make dead people alive. That is the Gospel. It is time to present the ultimate purpose in life: to follow Jesus wholeheartedly.

God has no grandchildren.

THE GREAT ADVENTURE

Life in Christ is the greatest adventure known to humankind. It costs everything. And the returns are so much more than the costs that we tend to forget. To be disengaged with purpose has caused many to wander to the enemy's camp because at least they get to be involved in his plan, although dark. It's time to get rearranged in our thinking, our values, and allow people to be shaped by life in the glory: revival. It's time to place our values in yet another Pentecost, one that confronts our misconceptions and restarts us in a direction that all of Heaven can say amen to, and at the same time wonder in amazement at. I have this sense that angels have been bored for a long time. And they are waiting for someone to live at a level of risk and pursuit of the impossible, that they finally have something worth doing on our behalf. Is this not their assignment? I think so.

Larry Sparks makes a profound statement in his book, *Ask for Rain:* "God's agenda for revival... is increasing Heaven's territory and jurisdiction on earth. As long as we are navigating revival correctly, stagnancy and sameness will be impossible."[3]

What a beautiful statement. Stagnancy and sameness will be impossible. So true. We need this kind of outpouring that makes religious form, instead of authentic Kingdom displays, impossible to dwell with us. It is time to come together, repenting of our differences and biases, and pray until He comes. And may we hear yet another *roar* from Heaven that releases a sound from our yielded hearts over our cities in a way that compels the unbeliever to come. And may we not be turned off by their offense and instead help them to discover why they heard the sound in the first place: The Father was drawing them to their destiny, which begins with faith in Christ.

This Spirit of revival, this baptism of fire, this that Jesus directed His disciples to pursue, is what the Father had promised. It comes as a gift from a perfect and wonderful Father, who only does wonderous things, who only gives good gifts to His children. "*Every good and perfect gift comes from the Father...*" (James 1:17). Perhaps if we viewed Pentecost as the ultimate Christmas morning, where together we open gifts from a Father whose delight in us is extreme and generous, then we could once again become like children and receive what He designed for our welfare and His glory.

I'm thankful for all we have seen and experienced, but I live aware of our need for the ever-increasing glory revealed in another Pentecost. More, Lord!

NOTES

1. Larry Sparks, comp., *Ask for the Rain: Receiving Your Inheritance for Revival & Outpouring*, (Shippensburg, PA: Destiny Image, 2016), 27.

2. Larry Sparks, comp., *Ask for the Rain: Receiving Your Inheritance for Revival & Outpouring*, (Shippensburg, PA: Destiny Image, 2016), 41.

3. Ibid.

Chapter Thirteen

REVIVAL, REFORMATION, AND RENAISSANCE

When revival itself becomes our goal, it is seldom attained because it becomes an idol. Revival must never become an end in itself, but a means to an even higher end—the glory of the lord being revealed and His kingdom being extended.

—RICK JOYNER[1]

RENAISSANCE is probably the most unusual term I could use for what reformation should lead us into. It's a positive term to some and questionable to others. There are good reasons on both sides of the issue. While that particular time in history was marked by great increase in the value for beauty and for human life, it also describes a period of time that gave rise to impurity and perversion. As we so often do, we tend to reject people and ideas if the enemy found a way to influence with his destruction. Sometimes people even disregard biblical characters like Solomon and Samson, or people of recent history whose lives ended in disgrace. But then the insights we often need the most are hidden in the lives of those who were used powerfully by God before compromise or destruction took them out. Paying attention to what brought their downfall is wisdom. But it's only fully effective if we're mindful of what brought about their success in the eyes of God in the first place.

Renaissance means "rebirth" or "reawakening" or even "revival." It is a beautiful term to describe how civilization came out of some very turbulent times and came more fully into God's delightful design for life in families and communities.

Let me briefly summarize this period that spanned around three hundred years as a God season, while attempting to do so by "eating the meat, and throwing out the bones."

The Renaissance was a passionate period of cultural, artistic, political and economic transformation that impacted all of Europe. It followed the Middle Ages, or as some would call it, the Dark Ages, the period that followed the downfall of the Roman Empire and was marked by political, economic, and cultural decline. While the Dark Ages seems to be mislabeled according to many historians, it will suffice in this very brief overview. Darkness did in fact prevail in many ways over society. Family life and community wellbeing were often buried in chaos, primarily through the loss of value for human life, exemplified by slavery and overall brutality toward others. And while there are flashes of light throughout that age, which is always connected somehow to the work of the wonderous Gospel, it was a dark season in its overall impact on history. But then something happened: A man named Marcilio Ficino inspired and directed dramatic change for countless numbers of people. He was a priest, a theologian, a philosopher, a linguist, among other amazing titles and accomplishments. And while he is not the only voice in this unique season, he is recognized as a primary figure. I mention him because his influence gave place to brilliance and beauty at previously unheard-of levels. I have several books that contain his letters to other contemporary thinkers of his day, including artists, priests, and other people of influence. And he was their inspiration.

I never cease to be amazed at how one person can be the catalyst of transformation, even for a whole continent. Such is the case for Marcilio Ficino.

My dear friend, Richard Chandler, who is a true student of Ficino, wanted to help me understand the impact of the simple but profound life of this humble man, as well as illustrate some of the fruit of his life (what his beliefs were "unto") and how we can apply his revelations to our own lives. Richard wrote:

> How can someone create their own Renaissance? I believe Ficino was highly intentional in how he worked to influence culture (but not the Church, which saw all new ideas as threats to their worldview) in the spheres of art, business, philosophy and health. He was concerned with, and had an advanced understanding for his time of, body, soul and spirit. [Even] his love for astrology...in my view... was Ficino's way of seeing God in all things, including the beauty of the solar system.
>
> Ficino translated Plato from Greek to Latin —"from old to new"— and with the new wineskin came a new vintage of wine, an application to his time and space. Plato may have sparked his thinking of a God-centric divine universe, but Ficino built new revelations. By doing so, he was able to bring society out of a monolithic Church age and ideology into a world of creativity (the Renaissance). He was not content to just enjoy his revelations—he worked to activate them within society. Ficino's "untos" included:

- Being a mentor to Lorenzo de Medici, aka "Lorenzo the Magnificent," who financed the most creative season of the Renaissance. In the House of the Medici, he played the role as priest, scholar, counsellor, philosopher and physician. This role gave him a platform for influence in business, politics and the arts. The Medici later financed his Academy of Florence.

- Counselling the artist Sandro Botticelli (painter of *The Birth of Venus* and *Primavera*).

- Establishing the Academy of Florence to train philosophical thought. His star student was Pico della Mirandola (who wrote the *Oration on the Dignity of Man*, a classic text on human rights).

- Influencing leaders across Europe with his letters. His letters attest to a gift of wisdom and word craftsmanship.

- Influencing the writer Baldassare Castiglione who wrote the book, *The Courtier*, which became famous across Europe, about how to educate a young prince in correct values and behaviors.

Richard added, "There is a reason he is the 'hidden' architect of the Renaissance. Humility led to revelation. Revelation led 'unto' legacy."

I understand that not everyone is interested in Ficino's impact on the Renaissance, especially those who burn for revival. And yet, it's the bigger picture that I desire to make all aware of. Seeing what cultural transformation looks like gives us the ability to endure past the ebbs and flows of the moves of God into that which has the ability to change the world. We never want to make society comfortable without God. Instead, all we do is to awaken the world to His voice, His purpose, and the overwhelming reason for which we are alive. This is true Renaissance. And it will happen again.

I also write this not so much to promote a man, Ficino, as noble and as worthwhile as that task may be. I write this to awaken those who have the same background as I do to the realization that there is more. More, in areas that we never thought possible. Transformation of culture is not merely to make everyone a powerful evangelist, as wonderful as that would be. It is rather to model the kind of life on earth that God intended in the first place. And that is the true power of evangelism. It draws people to Christ.

HUMANISM

Ficino is called a humanist by many historians. But the term *humanist*, as it is used to describe Ficino, is not the same as it is today. Today's humanist fights for life without Christ at the center, with no sense of responsibility and/or accountability. For many of them, people are their own god, and there is no design, purpose, or destiny beyond self-fulfillment and self-governance. For Ficino, this was unacceptable. He elevated the value for humanity back to its rightful place. He restored people to a place of personal dignity and celebrated the intellectual wonder of every human being. He explained what was the absolute truth that he lived from in his commentary on the *Symposium*. He wrote that the highest form of human love and friendship "is a communion based ultimately on the soul's love for God."[2] It is as though his value for human life and ingenuity was birthed in his joyous relationship with God, which is really only possible through Jesus Christ. His form of humanism emphasized the beauty of mankind as being *because of God,* and not *independent from God.* With that in mind, imagine a society where the love for people, beauty, and all creative expressions in commerce, education, health, and politics centered around loving God well. That is the real heart of the Renaissance. It is the celebration of a heart connection with God, and from there we have the privilege of living fully with divine purpose and design. This is a responsibility. And all responsibility in its nature implies accountability. Even in love we know that we will give an account of our lives to our loving Father.

THE THREEFOLD CORD

I've used three basic terms to describe the varieties, or unique expressions and impacts, of the moves of God: *revival, reformation,* and now *renaissance.* I don't want to make these terms too rigid, in the sense that they are stepping-stones of progress, i.e., first we have revival, and then turn it into a reformation, etc. These terms also shouldn't be exclusive, in that each realm has one specific fruit or result, as their similarities outweigh their differences.

Other great teachers, preachers, and authors may use any number of other equally significant terms to describe what we're experiencing, and the intended impact or result upon society. These come to mind: Renewal, Transformation, and Great Awakening. *Renewal* is often used to describe that which prepares us for revival. Both *Transformation* and *Great Awakening* are terms used to describe the impact of the move of God upon society, emphasizing our roles of influence as *salt, light, and leaven.* All three are excellent and useful terms and should be sought after in prayer and practice. I have used these words in my own teachings through the years and will continue to do so. But to simplify my message for this book, I chose to reduce our subject into these three overarching realms that represent most clearly what is in my heart. With that in mind, let's take another look at this idea:

- Revival reveals the holiness and power of God.

- Reformation reveals the heart and mind of God.

- Renaissance reveals the beauty and wonder of God.

I hope this becomes more and more clear, but we never fully leave one realm in order to enter another. Ultimately, all three can and should function at the same time. Let me put it this way, the most reliable and impacting approach is for us to honor the fires of revival, while advancing in the realms of influence of reformation, all the while growing in our approach to beauty, creativity, and wonder that is made possible through the influence of His overwhelming presence. In other words, we never lose our need for the fires of revival. If we see revival for what it is in the eyes of God, we would never seek to *mature our way beyond revival*. The other realms are made possible *because* of revival.

Living with all three realities firmly planted in our hearts and lifestyle is very much like the mystery of compound interest, which is where a financial investment increases exponentially, not just linearly. Let me explain. Consider for a moment how an investment earns income. And then, when that earned income remains invested, both the original investment, and the interest gained, increase the earning potential. This unending cycle is a key to great increase in the financial world. Albert Einstein is usually the one credited with the statement, "Compound interest is the eighth wonder of the world." This analogy fits perfectly with staying involved (invested) in each of the ever-increasing realms of God's grace, as He works His wonders in the Church and in society. Each area continues to bring income (spiritual riches and heavenly breakthroughs) and strengthens each of these three expressions of God's presence in the world.

AN INVITATION TO LEARN

My city is a small, mostly white community. We have certainly never been an international destination. Our culture, while beautiful, is very narrow in its expression. The great cultural centers of the world, as say New York City, or Toronto, have great beauty and class, largely because of their diversity. While I acknowledge Redding's being mostly white, it's not an accusation or complaint. It just is. But something beautiful has been happening here for the past 15 years, and especially in the past 5 to 10 years. We are being invaded by the nations. Let me explain. Our ministry school has had over 100 nations of the world come to this small town in Northern California to study in our school and take the culture of this house back to their churches and cities. What a privilege it has been for us. There are usually around 70 nations represented at one time through approximately 1000 international students. As you can probably imagine, that has changed the cultural landscape of this mostly white town that now has the beauty of diversity as a gift. Simpson University, also located in Redding, has a similar effect. The Bethel family not only has welcomed the nations with open arms; together, we celebrate the uniqueness each group brings. I'm happy to say that our city has also welcomed the diversity of races and cultures from the nations as well. And we are richer as a result.

Every year we have what's called The Festival of Cultures, in which many nations represented in our school set up booths to display the beauty of their nation through pictures, flags, and cultural items. The students from that nation also cook traditional foods for us to sample.

I must say it is a highlight of the year, attended with joy by about 1500 people.

ART IS NOT THE GOAL

Let's make something very clear: It would be foolish to emphasize the *art* of renaissance over *souls* changed in revival. That would be a misplacement of priorities. But in the same way that the art in the home is not more important than the walls or the foundation, it still is the art that reveals the values and nature of the owner. It was never meant to be a choice between one or the other. Winning souls for Christ is the priority. But beauty is to line the halls of the journey. Misplaced priorities, like art above souls, have caused many to ignore or devalue these elements even when they are in their rightful place. The error of others causes many to fear getting it wrong, more than they see the benefit of getting it right.

In an unusual illustration of this concept, Israel took the bronze serpent that Moses made and worshipped it. That serpent was a tool that God used for their healing in the wilderness. It was a gift from God. But when they worshipped it, they exalted it above the place that God intended, and it became a snare to them. And Hezekiah destroyed it.

> *He removed the high places and broke the sacred pillars, cut down the wooden image and broke in pieces the bronze serpent that Moses had made; for until those days the children of Israel burned incense to it, and called it Nehushtan* (2 Kings 18:4).

So it is with so many things in the Kingdom. Eternity with God, through salvation in Jesus Christ alone, is preeminent. But there are other areas of importance that must be embraced and enjoyed as parts of this life of salvation. Jesus taught us to honor our father and mother. But He goes on to say that those who love father or mother more than Him are not worthy of Him. Gifts from God, from spouses and family, to jobs, provisions, and favor, are all to aid us in our affectionate journey of loving God well. Each element is to remind us of His goodness and His favor upon us. Each in their place enhances our relationship with God. Out of place, it undermines that same relationship.

Exalting art, commerce, politics, and the like above the salvation of souls is foolish at best. But salvation is to look like something. I realize that for many, being soul-winners is what the convert's life is to look like. But there's more. God is the best cook, tailor, actor, businessman, musician, farmer, doctor, lawyer, and on and on the list goes. The point is, when we step into our design and purpose, we reveal Him. Our cities are to be filled with the joyful presence of people who have found their purpose. Such a life declares the covenant, nature, and presence of God to all who will listen. This divine encounter is available to all who know us. It is the message that invites people into a relationship with God, where life on earth makes sense and is filled with purpose, design, and adventure.

THE VALUE OF BEAUTY

In his book, *Beauty Will Save the World*, author Brian Zahnd repeats an important story from Church history, which he mentioned in his prelude. A thousand years ago, Prince Vladimir the Great was looking for a new religion that might unite his people. Although he, himself, was a heathen, he recognized that spirituality might bring his people together in a common bond. He sent delegations into the neighboring countries to examine their religions and the effect on their lives. The envoy to examine Christianity went to the Byzantine capital of Constantinople. Below is his response:

> Then we went to Constantinople and they led us to the place where they worship their God, and we knew not whether we were in heaven or earth, for on earth there is no such vision nor beauty, and we do not know how to describe it; we only know that God dwells among men. We cannot forget that beauty.

This is a testimony to the power of beauty. The words of these delegates were in response to the Christians' worship of God and to the aesthetic beauty of their surroundings that they created to honor God. This beauty won their hearts. Heathens were drawn to God because there was a generation given the liberty to create beauty wherever they had influence. This gift of creative expression is meant to reveal the nature of God. As such, it reveals Him and has an effect on people's awareness of the heart of God.

Creative expression is meant

to reveal the nature of God.

WHAT WAS GOD THINKING?

God has very different ways of addressing problems than we would. His solutions reveal His unique perception of the unseen world, while at the same time putting us in a place of having to trust Him completely. Here are a few fascinating examples:

- God had the musicians and singers lead the way into war. (See Second Chronicles 20.)

- God used musical instruments (tambourines and harps) to bring destruction on the enemy. (See Isaiah 30:32.)

- God had Moses raise his hands so Israel would win a war. (See Exodus 17:11.)

- God said a shout of joy would cure barrenness. (See Isaiah 54:1.)

- God used a boy's lunch to feed thousands. (See John 6.)

Of course, the Bible is filled with such stories. What is fun to see is that these realities reveal the logic of God. He thinks differently because He sees completely. He sees the beginning from the end. He sees the unseen realms clearer than we see the visible. All the laws of the unseen realm come from His nature and abilities. The stories of Scripture remind us that He often uses things we would not consider powerful through which to display His power. I can't think of many other examples that are any more extreme in displaying that truth than the following:

Then I raised my eyes and looked, and there were four horns. And I said to the angel who talked with me, "What are these?"

*So he answered me, "These are the horns that have scattered Judah, Israel, and Jerusalem." Then the Lord showed me **four craftsmen**. And I said, "What are these coming to do?" So he said, "These are the horns that scattered Judah, so that no one could lift up his head; but the **craftsmen** are coming to terrify them, to cast out the horns of the nations that lifted up their horn against the land of Judah to scatter it"* (Zechariah 1:18-21 NKJV).

Here we see a spiritual conflict between the powers of darkness and the people of God. Horns represent strength and authority in Scripture. This prophesy reveals that four realms of power or authorities will rise up in the earth to divide and destroy the people of God. The number four often represents the world, or the natural realm as we know it, as in the four directions on a compass, north, south, east, and west, or as in the phrase, *the four corners of the earth.* The spiritual entities spoken of by Zechariah become successful in their attempts to destroy by scattering God's people. This is a direct assault on community and family life, the bedrock of how our identity is displayed. The impact of these spiritual beings is devastation and worldwide (as the number four represents *all over the earth.*) But then, God has an answer to this problem, which is also worldwide, represented again by the number four. His plan was to raise up and release four *artisans*, or *craftsmen*. I don't believe this is referring to four individual people any more than the four horns mentioned are only four people. It instead represents a global movement, or even a *grace* that comes upon the people of God, which in turn encompasses the whole world. The word *artisans* speaks of a worldwide realm of creative expression that is anointed by God to forcefully deal with the powers of darkness that are seeking to kill, steal, and destroy. Amazing. First it was choirs sent into battle, and now creative expression is used to destroy the powers of darkness and the plans of the evil one. Perhaps we can see through this divine value why the powers of darkness always try to keep the people of God in fear and anxiety. These things war against the creative expression that God intends to flow through us. And the devil does not want the creative and joyful nature of God to be seen through the people of God. Such a display of who God is, and what He is like, will automatically spread to the nations of the world. The hunger for such things comes from the vacuum in the consciousness of humanity of God's goodness.

It is normal for us to wonder how God could make the creative expressions of the people of God supernaturally powerful. Consider this picture that is given to us by the prophet Isaiah:

> *And in every place where the staff of punishment passes,*
> *Which the Lord lays on him,*
> *It will be with tambourines and harps;*
> *And in battles of brandishing He will fight with it* (Isaiah 30:32).

I absolutely love verses like this. They challenge my reasoning, which needs to be challenged. He thinks completely differently from me, and I'm the one that must change. Reality is redefined in moments like these, as we see the effect of the unseen world on the visible. What is remarkable to me in this passage is that we are the ones playing the musical instrument, yet it is as though the Lord is the one playing. He uses our surrendered efforts that are illustrated in obedience and makes them supernaturally effective against the enemy. The picture is of the Lord punishing the powers of darkness with each strum of the harp or each beat on the tambourine. It is His partnership with us that makes what we do powerful.

The powers that had weakened the people of God through scattering are dealt with thoroughly through the influence of craftsmen, who take their place in society. Is it possible that art, beauty and the corresponding joy have this kind of impact on the unseen world today? I think so. God is restoring us to the standards of the Renaissance, where human life is restored to great value. This is and will be measurable by doing away with abortion, slavery, racism, sex trafficking, etc.

It goes beyond the obvious offenses a criminal brings to society and regains a value in the potential rehabilitation of the prisoner. From there they're released back into society to be a contributor, not a destroyer. Isn't this included in the announcement of what Jesus came for? Isn't that His own description of what the anointing of the Holy Spirit looks like when it rests upon the Son of God? Prisoners are released, the blind see, and the brokenhearted are healed. This is the exact moment where the prophet announced that cities are to be restored to beauty and function. And this is where the most broken among us become the trophies of God's grace, whom He then uses to rebuild the destroyed cities that they once lived in to destabilize. This is the heart, plan, and promise of God. As such, it must have influence on our value of people, beauty, community life, and our own unique expression is whatever assignment we have received in life.

JESUS, PERFECT THEOLOGY

Read these verses carefully. It's quite possible that we have become overly familiar with them and are no longer wowed by their significance. They describe the merging of these three realms, three movements, and these three areas of legacy in God: revival that reveals holiness and power, reformation that introduces us to God's heart and wisdom, and renaissance, which restores us to beauty and wonder. And all of this is found in the person of Jesus, who described the wonderful impact of the Holy Spirit resting upon Him. Should we expect anything less when He rests upon us?

The Spirit of the Lord God is upon Me,

Because the Lord has anointed Me

To preach good tidings to the poor;

He has sent Me to heal the brokenhearted,

To proclaim liberty to the captives,

And the opening of the prison to those who are bound;

To proclaim the acceptable year of the Lord,

And the day of vengeance of our God;

To comfort all who mourn,

To console those who mourn in Zion,

To give them beauty for ashes,

The oil of joy for mourning,

The garment of praise for the spirit of heaviness;

That they may be called trees of righteousness,

The planting of the Lord, that He may be glorified.

And they shall rebuild the old ruins,

They shall raise up the former desolations,

And they shall repair the ruined cities,

The desolations of many generations (Isaiah 61:1-4).

The most wonderful conclusion to this portion of Scripture is the cities that have been in ruins for many generations are brought back to beauty, order and life. This is a miracle as much as any seen in Scripture. And it's accomplished by the ones who were the most broken and despised through their own issues, i.e. prisoners. The effects of the working of the Holy Spirit, through miracles, politics, as well as the realms of beauty and design, all work to reveal God. As we discover God—His nature, presence, and covenant—we discover why we're alive, and what we can contribute to the overall story of humanity on planet Earth.

It's very important to recognize that the touch of beauty in life does not rest upon the shoulders of artists, architects and musicians alone. Art, in a very real sense in the Kingdom, is the way we approach life itself. There are unique expressions and creative ways of doing things that accountants, doctors, and lawyers have access to. Stay-at-home moms or dads can also live with access to the creative ideas that make life an adventure. If there is one thing that children are known for, it is love for adventure. And maturity, for us, is to be childlike. All of this speaks of the whole realm of adventure and creativity that is to be associated with following Christ.

HUMAN LIFE 101

Restoring the value for human life is one of the profound effects of the Renaissance grace or anointing. All of the manifestations of the graces of God must be detectible through measurable outcomes. For example, our love for God is to be measured in our love for people. To hate people and love God is a contradiction. It is impossible. The value for human life changes in revival, reformation, and renaissance.

Another way to say it is that the value for human life changes under the full effect of the Gospel:

— The Unborn —

Abortion is the equivalent of the sacrifice of children to the god Molech. Because it has been around for a while, we have become accustomed to it. Even many who oppose it out of principle are no longer appalled. We have a mandate to stand for biblical justice, which is to stand up for those who have no voice. And no group of people has less of a voice than the unborn. Renaissance, in its purist form, changes this issue from a political matter to a moral one. When life is valued and celebrated, we no longer look for chances to benefit from another's loss, as is the convenient context of aborting a child who will no longer make demands on a person's life.

Our love for God is to be measured

in our love for people.

— Sex Trafficking —

It is strange to see how common sex trafficking has become and how ignorant we are as a society to this travesty. Our numbness to this issue is the result of a deadening of our God-given discernment, which happens through the barrage of sexualizing of everything from toothpaste to cars, to the daily diet of soft-porn on the average TV show. What was once easy to recognize has become more and more difficult to detect. The enemy has sponsored an all-out effort to culturize the Church to make us relevant. Sin and the unrenewed mind only make us relevant to the culture of darkness. What is portrayed in entertainment that has become acceptable has cost us dearly.

— The Poor —

We have multiple reactions to caring for the poor, usually based on experience and failed government programs. In my circles, everyone wants to care for the poor. No one wants them left in their poverty. But the question is, how do we fix the problem? Throwing money at the problem won't fix it. But neither will the problem be solved without throwing money at it. My favorite verse on the subject is in Proverbs 13:23:

> *Abundant food is in the fallow ground of the poor, but it is swept away by injustice.*

Abundance is within reach of the poor. But injustice interferes with their process of obtaining it. Injustice affects their sowing and reaping and the God-given knowledge to make wealth. Justice is rarely self-initiated. It must be championed by another on their behalf. For this reason, poverty is everyone's problem, not just the government's.

— The Elderly —

Instead of merely tolerating those who are no longer productive nor able to contribute to society, honor and celebrate them because of their lives that paved a way for our own success. Honor is central, which is difficult for societies that determine a person's value by what they generate through their success. The answer is not another government program. The answer is the value we have on those who have spent themselves for the sake of this generation. Our commitment must be to work for the quality of life for those unable to contend for themselves.

— The Afflicted —

This area covers the sick, physically challenged and mentally deficient. It is not a burden on society to care for those who can't take care of themselves. It is an honor. Instead of drugging them beyond coherency, we have the privilege of finding a way to care for those unable to provide for themselves and bring the best quality of life that the person in question is capable of enjoying.

> *Give strong drink to him who is perishing,*
> *And wine to those who are bitter of heart.*
> *Let him drink and forget his poverty,*
> *And remember his misery no more* (Proverbs 31:6-7 NKJV).

Obviously, this verse is not condoning alcoholism or drunkenness. It is instead a declaration of the privileged responsibility to care for those who are dying and bitter (discontented) of heart. It's what kings do. It's what we naturally do for others when we're not fighting for our own identity and position in life. These really are the expressions of a culture of confidence in divine purpose and assertion of the value of the individual.

— Races and Cultures —

Diversity is beautiful. It is necessary. In fact, my approach is that without diversity, there can be no biblical unity. Each race and culture is to be celebrated. Racism is evil. It is demonic to its core. To treat people with dishonor because of their skin color is absolute foolishness. To turn that dishonor into violence is barbaric and inhuman. In Christ, we have the privilege and responsibility to oppose racism in all its forms and stand with those who have suffered under its weight. Sometimes taking the time to hear of the history of another helps us to understand where they are coming from and the why of their reactions to civil issues. My dad used to tell us, "When you wash the feet of another, you find out why they walk the way they do." This is brilliant and true.

Without diversity,
there can be no biblical unity.

— Miscellaneous —

There are many other people groups, and areas of life that deserve mentioning in this context. My list was never meant to be complete. It is a sample list that represents the nature of impact that the Renaissance grace is to have on the world around us. This is the beauty of the Renaissance.

This brings us to the foundation of the Renaissance: righteousness and justice. Everything listed above becomes a successful expression in society if there are these two elements. Think through this with me. The Renaissance is all about beauty, design and the restoration of the value for human life to society. In my way of thinking, renaissance is all about freedom: the freedom to become all that God intended and the freedom to express all that God has put within us. I once heard it said that, "Freedom is not being able to do whatever I want. Freedom is the ability to do what is right." That is true freedom indeed. Freedom is the grace to become and explore through a childlike passion for adventure. Righteousness and justice are the foundation of the throne of God and of every throne on earth that is to have lasting and life-giving impact.

THE CONFLICT

I don't know of any leader in the Church that doesn't delight in the fulfilled vision of the people they serve. Perhaps it's the friend with the new restaurant that is packed out every night. Or maybe it's the single mom who found a new apartment closer to work. And then there's the professional athlete who signed a significant new contract that brings blessing to their family and beyond. And while the application for this concept is different in the villages of Africa or the favelas in Brazil, the excitement of spiritual leaders over the increase and blessing of others remains the same.

While the concept of progress or promotion is acceptable for the individuals we serve or even in the life of a church family, it is all too rarely thought to be a part of our commission from the Lord for cities and then nations.[3] For some reason, nationwide peace and blessing are thought to be the result of the false narrative coming from the anti-Christ or some other false hope for the world. For this reason, the people who tend to walk with the greatest power and have the opportunity to have the greatest impact on humanity assume that it is an error to hope for lasting peace for a generation. Such hope seems to war in our minds with the legitimate desire for the Lord's return.

My friend and associate, Kris Vallotton, illustrates this challenge brilliantly:

> What we believe about the end has a lot to do with how we behave in the middle. For example, say I have a 1955 Chevy, and you have an automotive restoration shop. Imagine that I take my car into your shop to be rebuilt from the ground up and I inform you that money is no object. But in the middle of the restoration project, you discover that I am going to enter the old Chevy in the destruction derby after you complete the project. That information is definitely going to affect the quality of your work!
>
> In the same way, any reasonable person should be able to figure out that their end-time perspective can dramatically affect the quality of their daily lives. Once again, Isaiah prophesied that the Spirit of the Lord has anointed us to see freedom and restoration come into people's lives and described how their personal restoration would result in cities and nations being rebuilt. He wrote, "Then they will rebuild the ancient ruins, they will raise up the former devastations; and they will repair the ruined cities, the desolations of many generations" (Isaiah 61:4). It is difficult to feel empowered to restore ruined cities and at the same time believe that the condition of the world needs to

erode for Jesus to return. Can you see that our eschatology is actually working against our ministry?[4]

HOPE, OUR ETERNAL MANDATE

Without hope, we are a pitiful people. We follow religious routines, wanting something good to happen as a result. Hope, on the other hand, is anchored in the Word of God. It is founded upon His nature that is manifested in the covenant made with His people. Perhaps this is why the word used in Scripture actually means "the joyful anticipation of good." By nature, hope creates the context for faith to function in. When we live fueled by such hope, we become infectious. And if there is anything people are wanting in this time, it is a reason to hope. We, the people of God, are to be the most hopeful people on earth. Our hope is not hope in humanity. It is not hope in our personal gifts or vision. It is hope in the purposes of God, revealed in and through His people. This is our hour to stand tall, realizing that *"God so loved the world, that He gave His only begotten Son."* He is the foundation of all hope. Perhaps living under the influence of His heart and mind would make us the people of influence that God designed in the first place. This is our hour. *"Arise and shine, for your light has come"* (Isa. 60:1).

We, the people of God, are to be

the most hopeful people on earth.

NOTES

1. Rick Joyner, *The World Aflame: The Welsh Revival and Its Lessons for Our Time* (Fort Mill, SC: Morningstar Publications, 2013), 29.

2. Britannica, The Editors of Encyclopaedia. "Marsilio Ficino." Encyclopedia Britannica, 15 Oct. 2020, https://www.britannica.com/biography/Marsilio-Ficino. Accessed 27 January 2021.

3. I dealt with this subject much more thoroughly in my book, *Born for Significance* (Lake Mary, FL: Charisma House, 2020).

4. Kris Vallotton, *Heavy Rain: Reforming the Church to Transform the World* (Regal, 2010).

Chapter Fourteen

A MATURE MAN

Revival is God's arrival! And though we rejoice in what
we have already received in the provision of Christ,
we yet long for the full equipping. . . (from the) five-
fold ministries who will bring us into the experiential
wonder of the fullness of the Son of God.
—LOU ENGLE[1]

THIS is the final chapter of *Open Heavens*. And as strange as it
may seem, I want to conclude this book on revival in a most
unusual place: the wonder, beauty, and maturity planned for the
entire Body of Christ. *A mature man* is the biblical description of the
Church I just described. It portrays the Body of Christ in a way that we
could all hope for, but could in no way make happen. With each passing
year it seems more and more impossible. And yet it is real, as it is the
heart of God. And because He declared it, it is possible.

The Bible creates a picture of the last-days Church that is in a place of
maturity in unity, purity, strength, and function. Quite honestly, what God
has in mind is beyond what any of us would have the intelligence to ask for.

I know very few pastors and leaders who believe that this will happen
before Jesus returns. And while it is impossible for us, it is not impossible

for Him. The idea that this kind of maturity could happen in eternity or the millennium reveals that we have more faith in the return of Christ than we do in the power of the Gospel. And that's nothing to be proud of. I hope to instill hope in His plan, process, and ability to bring it about.

EMBRACE THE PROCESS

The process for this impossible feat is one we can enjoy and celebrate now. God created a method to bring about this dream, desire, or conclusion. It is the function of what we typically call the fivefold ministry. It is simple. It is profound. It will work.

> And **He gave** some as apostles, and some as prophets, and some as evangelists, and some as pastors and teachers, **for the equipping** of the saints for the work of service, to the building up of the body of Christ; **until** we all attain to the unity of the faith, and of the knowledge of the Son of God, to **a mature man**, to the measure of the stature which belongs to the **fullness of Christ** (Ephesians 4:11-13).

What makes this passage an uphill battle for the Church to accept and believe is that we often live in reaction to what we have seen misused: in this case, inappropriate titles, along with self-promotion. I'm sure all of us have had our fill of those who call themselves apostle, prophet, or whatever sounds lofty to them. And yet these offices still exist, according to the will and design of God, the perfect creator. Their value and significance are becoming more and more clear, as the outcome spoken of by Paul cannot be accomplished any other way. These insights were given by the apostle Paul to the Church known for revival (Acts 19) and known for wisdom and great maturity. (See Revelation 2:2-3.) In other words, this instruction was given to a people already living in a realm of glory, which is life in revival. He did this to equip them with wisdom to go to the next level.

The apostle, prophet, evangelist, pastor, and teacher each carried an aspect of Jesus' personal ministry for the benefit of the Church, which is people. I don't personally care if I'm given a title or not. But I do want to function in what I believe the call of God is for my life. I do think it is somewhat humorous to see the reaction of people to an individual with the title *apostle*, while no one reacts to the title *pastor*. The term or office of pastor is rarely mentioned in Scripture while the word apostle(s) is mentioned over 70 times. We may need to get over our biases and/or fears to go where He wants us to go.

Have I seen people who claimed to be apostles that were not? Yes, I sure have. But I've honestly seen more people who claimed to be pastors, who were not. Instead of worrying about titles and such, let's consider the full and proper function of these five gifts to be the *secret sauce* of God's recipe for transformation. It is in the role of these five that we see a more complete representation of the heart and will of God for His people, and through them it will affect planet Earth.

DISCOVERING WHY

Each of these gifts/ministries was to equip the saints to perform the work of ministry as modeled by Jesus. All areas of ministry were to be carried out by the members of the church. Each of the various roles, from the prophetic to the evangelistic, to the loving care of the pastor for the sheep, and beyond, was to flow naturally because people were thoroughly equipped to do it and do it well. This process of living in the flow of the life of Christ through us was an exercise that resulted in building up the Body, which is the Church. The effect on all of us is the same way a weight lifter would build up their body through exercise. This process of learning to do what the Father is doing and say what He is saying is the ultimate exercise in true spirituality. It doesn't happen instead of pursuing our personal relationship with Jesus; it happens because of it. This lifestyle introduces us to the God of the impossible and takes us into a vital place of trust, if we're to actually go where this passage, Ephesians 4:11-13, promises. Our proper function in life is to perfect and strengthen the Church in faith, anointing, and ability to impact the world around them. Imagine Christ, multiplied by millions called Christians who are having an impact on the world around them through faithful service in power and purity as Jesus did. That was the plan, and that is what He enabled us to do through the fivefold ministry of Jesus flowing through people.

This process of learning to do what the Father is doing and say what He is saying is the ultimate exercise in true spirituality.

GRACE MAKES THE IMPOSSIBLE POSSIBLE

To benefit fully from this concluding chapter, we need a little better understanding of grace. Seeing grace accurately will help us to focus our attention and efforts toward utilizing a profound gift that is right in front of us most of our lives though we all too often live unaware of it.

Most of us know the word *grace* by this common but beautiful definition, "the unmerited favor of God." This explanation is absolutely true, and must be celebrated as such. But that definition is also incomplete. Paul gives us greater understanding of this word through his use of it in Ephesians when he describes himself and his responsibilities.

> *I was made a minister, according to the gift of God's grace which was given to me according to the working of His power. To me, the very least of all saints, this grace was given, to preach to the Gentiles the unfathomable riches of Christ, and to bring to light what is the administration of the mystery which for ages has been hidden in God who created all things; so that the manifold wisdom of God might now be made known through the church to the rulers and the authorities in the heavenly places* (Ephesians 3:7-10).

If we examine these few verses, we can see that there are two benefits, or effects, of grace that can help us fulfill our destinies in Christ. The first is in verse 7, where he states that he was made a minister according to the gift of grace. To put it another way, Paul was turned into something according to the gift of grace. This process reminds me of a potter's hands, shaping clay. Grace fashioned him; it became the expression of God's hands in shaping who He designed Paul to be. Grace shapes our identity, for our destiny is possible only because of favor. But the second verse adds another insight for our lives that is becoming more and more essential: For Paul it was grace that enabled him to preach. Another way to say it is that grace enabled him to function in his assignment.

Grace creates *identity* for us, and grace enables us to *function* in our assignment. What we become and how we are to live are shaped and inspired by grace. *Grace* is "the enabling presence of God."

Grace is "the enabling presence of God."

How and why does this matter when we talk about the fivefold ministries? Because the key to this process is revealed in Ephesians 4:7, *"But to each one of us grace was given according to the measure of Christ's gift."* The gifts of Christ are the fivefold ministries. The enabling presence of God called *grace*, that the members of the Body are to receive for this humanly impossible destiny, in part comes through these gifts. If I don't receive from the gifts God placed in my life, then I will miss out on the level of identity and enablement He had purposed for me.

There are three ways, as I understand it, to receive grace. First is directly from the Lord in our relationship with Him. The second is from members of the Body, as in Ephesians 4:29. But the third, and the subject of this chapter, is through those who have been assigned by God to function as an apostle, prophet, evangelist, pastor, or teacher. These are offices, assigned by God, that exist for a particular function. Everyone can prophesy, but not all are prophets. All are to do the work of an evangelist, but not all are evangelists, etc.

The gifts of Christ equip the saints with grace. But it is done according to the measure of Christ's gift. In other words, what is the measure of the fivefold ministry that has input into the life of the average believer? The measure of the level of influence His gifts have, determines the measure of grace we live in. I look at it like fuel. I want my fuel tanks full for the journey He has assigned for me. For example, some people only listen to and receive from evangelists. That means they will have a strength in their lives for that particular area of ministry, but they will be less capable of functioning in the other areas of life that are required if we're going to really re-present Jesus.

Here is a simple definition of the grace given by the gifts of Christ:

> The grace of the apostle enables one to see the blueprint of Heaven for how we do life in a way that impacts culture.
>
> The grace of the prophet enables the believer to live more aware of the unseen with greater conviction and clarity.
>
> The grace of the evangelist enables the believer to see the value of a soul and carry out in an effective way the commission to make disciples.
>
> The grace of the pastor enables a believer to care for the needs of others and serve them with eternity in mind.
>
> The grace of a teacher enables a believer to approach the Word of God with diligence and passion that they might clearly understand and communicate the truth of God in love.

The purpose of the fivefold ministry is that they all equip the believer to properly function in a way that is consistent with the grace for the office they carry.

THE JOURNEY

The prophetic statement in Ephesians 4:13 is clear: *"until we all attain."*

The word *until* is critical to see and understand. Jesus set something in motion that will not stop *until.* In other words, the function of these particular gifts will not cease until they have accomplished God's intended purpose.

The *until we all attain* journey is much like a train on a railroad track; you can stop it, you can even go backwards, but you can't change the direction of the tracks themselves. We are all on a journey, a railroad track if you will, and that is to take us to the place where we *attain* something valuable to God. His desire is that the people of God would demonstrate the wonder and beauty of who Jesus is, again, worldwide. This is something from which God will be glorified: the Church, functioning in perfect alignment and cooperation with the head, Jesus Christ.

The first destiny mentioned in this journey is the *unity of faith.* Unity is not uniformity. In fact, unity by nature is complete only when there's diversity. It is made possible in the glory, which is the manifested presence of Jesus. (See John 17:22.) Biblical unity is humanly impossible. His goal is the unity of faith, not the unity of doctrine. One of the great dreams of the Church is for us to function as one in our expression of faith, in the same way that Jesus did, exactly. Remember, Jesus set the pattern for what is valuable to the Father. The unity of faith is to reveal and reinforce that which Jesus established as the way we do life, the way we do ministry.

Unity is not uniformity.

The second step in the journey is *the knowledge of the Son of God.* Can you imagine having all believers with the same, and/or complementary perspectives and perceptions of Jesus, the Son of God? This is the ambition of the Father, for if we get that one reality wrong, it affects everything else. If we see Him more clearly, we'll worship Him more extravagantly. It's automatic. And we always become like whatever we worship. Jesus must be seen for who He is, accurately, by all who have salvation in His name. Christlikeness is the outcome of *the knowledge of the Son of God.* Without this one breakthrough, we can never perfectly *re*-present Jesus. He is the desire of the nations, and without a clear manifestation of who He is, the nations will never find their purpose and destiny in Him. Finding it is the result of the knowledge of the Son of God.

We always become like whatever we worship.

THE GRAND FINALE

The goal of the Father is so far beyond what we would ever have the faith to ask for, or the intelligence to perceive. He has set us on a track that is headed toward our being *a mature man.* The plan of the Father is to turn us (all believers) into *a mature man,* singular. The whole Body of many members is to function as one, under the head, Christ Jesus. And through the mature Body of believers that cover the earth, Jesus is revealed again. This is the measure of the stature belonging to the fullness of Christ.

I want you to imagine something, but this time imagine as a dreamer: the Church, the Body of Christ, rising to a place of purity and power, in unity, to the point that we appear as one mature man. God's house is always designed to be filled with glory. How much more when it is the house He is building. The Church. The beauty of such unity is to include liturgical churches with Pentecostal churches, the safe church on main street in small town America, to the persecuted Church in places all over the globe. We are one body and members of one another. That is how He describes us. It's time that we become in our function what He says we are by our position. It must be possible this side of Heaven, or Paul's instruction is useless for now. What would it be like for us to live as one coordinated human body, like that of an athlete, to illustrate the wonder of Jesus Christ through the proper function of His Body? I'm not looking for human perfection. I'm looking for the perfect will of God. To have this happen worldwide is beyond astonishing. But it is possible simply because He declared it. It is His desire and plan.

If *a mature man* wasn't enough of a goal and target, he adds another layer by saying, *"to the measure of the stature which belongs to the fullness of Christ."* Think of it: the people of God, on earth, would completely illustrate and model *the fullness of Christ!* To fully illustrate Him will take the whole Church, not one person or even a stream or a movement.

DRINK OF HIS LOVE

The love of God for us is the single great reality in our lives. And if I live unaware of this reality, I will live too aware of all that is inferior.

The love of God is a well that we are to drink from, continually. It will help us to more naturally portray and manifest Jesus Christ, the glorious One, more fully.

Here's another statement made by Paul to this mature group of believers in Ephesus: *"to know the love of Christ which surpasses knowledge, that you may be filled up to all the fullness of God"* (Eph. 3:19). There are billions of universes in existence that we already know of right now. And there's so much more. They are all in the palm of His hand. Keep that in mind when you read of His intention to fill us with His fullness. No wonder our experience surpasses knowledge. In the original language, this verse is basically saying that "we are to know by experience, what is beyond comprehension." My heart will always take me where my head can't fit.

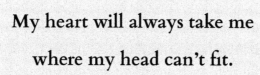

My heart will always take me
where my head can't fit.

REVIVAL, REFORMATION, AND RENAISSANCE

These three areas that have been the subject or target of this book, need to be addressed one last time, but this time through the lenses of the Ephesians 4:11-13 passage. As a reminder, I don't want to make these three realities too rigid, in that we think of them as stepping-stones. They have a natural overlap, and in part must be valued all at the same time. But for study's sake, I address them individually and run them through a filter created by this passage: We are given *equipment*, for a specific *function*, and in order to have a predetermined *outcome*.

Revival introduces us to the holiness and power of God. The grace given by the fivefold ministries equips us to walk in purity while at the same time demonstrating the power of God. Just as holiness was not to be experienced by only those who fill an office of Christ's gift (a fivefold ministry gift) neither was power ever meant to function in their lives alone. As John Wimber would say, "Everyone gets to play." The proper function of these gifts in the church enables us to come to a unity in our faith. And that unity of faith must spill out into the streets, as true revival reaches far beyond the gatherings in our meeting rooms. That's what happens when everyone is equipped to do the work of service—the work of revival. The unity of faith must also be for the miracles that bring glory to the name of Jesus. Perhaps this is also how we can imagine functioning more completely in this role as we model the fullness of Christ through our lives. What does that look like? I'm not sure completely. But it should at least bring back to the forefront the fact that Jesus healed and brought deliverance to everyone who came to Him needing His touch. Plus, He healed and delivered everyone the Father directed Him to. How could we manifest Him fully, as Paul states, and not have it include this part of His life? I also have a sense that for us to succeed in *the measure of the stature which belongs to the fullness of Christ"* (Eph. 4:13) we will need divine encounters as recorded in Jesus' Mount of Transfiguration experience. There is more than we can imagine or think of as it pertains to the fullness of Christ.

Reformation introduces us to the heart and mind of God. The gifts of Christ release grace into the Body of Christ, that we might carry the heart of God for cities and nations. Too often, our goals have more to do with our image of success as a ministry or church family, when in fact our success is measured by the impact outside of our gatherings. In reformation, people have permission to care and interact with community leaders, in everything from coaching little league to running for mayor. The *unity of our* faith is to have a measurable impact. The point is, the fivefold ministry is to equip people to become the spear point in the reformation of society. Permission must be given, training must take place, and people must be released into their destiny, without the church leaders becoming insecure by not being the center of all Christian activities. When we create a culture of permission, we free people to dream in a way that we would never dream ourselves. Suddenly, the wisdom of God becomes the most transferable part of our lives, as we impart the ability to *reign in life* to all who will be inspired by our example and our instruction from God's Word. This *fullness of Christ* makes us a wonderful gift to the city in a way that they value. We become like salt to a meal, in that we are to add to and enhance the flavor of the meal called Redding. (Insert the name of your city.) We are not the meal! We enhance what God has already designed for our cities and nations to be. As leaders, we rule to protect and serve to empower. That is the function of the gifts of Christ. They can and must lead us to a reformation where the compassion and wisdom of God are clearly seen in how we live our lives.

Renaissance introduces us to the wonder and beauty of God. One of the saddest parts of Church history is to see that oftentimes the most stationary, static part of our society is the Church, whose mantra has become, "We've never done it that way before." Change is resisted, almost always. It is inconsistent with our nature in Christ that the sons of daughters of the Creator become the most fearful when it's time to create. The fivefold ministry of Christ is to clear up this log jam in people's thinking. This problem is usually propagated by the leaders who become stagnant in their personal journey of faith. If we're not taking risks, we're probably not confronting our bent toward stagnation in pursuing comfort and ease of life as a priority. The gifts of Christ are responsible to equip and inspire people to experience their own creative juices. That is consistent with the nature of their heavenly Father. They inherited this when they were born again. Creativity in the arts and business, witty inventions, new ways to educate children, and creative solutions for the politicians who are called to serve humanity are all normal through the proper equipping of the saints. The point is, it's the gifts of Christ who equip, and give permission, vision, and divine grace to carry out this wonderful privilege of adding the beauty and wonder of God back into our daily lives and in turn, back into our world. The fullness of Christ is beyond significant. It must include the restoration of wonder. Today people wonder whether or not they'll have a job next month, or whether there will be more riots, or maybe they'll wonder about if there'll be another international crisis. The beauty and wonder we are to restore to society will free them to consider God, the Father and sustainer of life, the One who loves unconditionally, the One who is intensely committed to our wellbeing. This One is full of wonder. Gazing at Him spills over into our fascination in the beauty and wonder of God's most perfect creation: people. Celebrating humanity as an expression of the value we place in God Himself is vital. Everything He made, He acknowledged as good. But after creating man, He said it was "very good." Of course, people must be born again. That is the prize. But people tend to already know what's wrong with their lives. What they don't know is how God fashioned them for His glory. What they don't know is that this wonderful life is to be the beginning of eternity, where we will enjoy His gracious rule, forever. Jesus died a brutal death to make eternal wonder even possible.

God reveals what is possible in our lifetime just to make us hungry.

THE CRESCENDO

God reveals what is possible in our lifetime just to make us hungry. Hungry people impose restrictions upon themselves equal to their hunger. The absence of hunger for His will on earth causes us to wander carelessly, without restraints.

> *Where there is no revelation, the people cast off restraint; But happy is he who keeps the law* (Proverbs 29:18 NKJV).

The outpourings of the Holy Spirit make us more complete in every way.

Revelation here means *prophetic insight* into the heart and mind of God. It is a glimpse into His will, or more specifically His dream or desire. The implication is that if I have a prophetic glimpse into what God desires to do, I will become hungry for it. It is my nature to respond that way. And in that hunger, I will impose restrictions upon myself to give myself fully to what God has promised. Restrictions are not punishments, nor is the focus on what we can't have. The single-mindedness of this moment is so completely on the heart of God in a matter that we pull our efforts and energies away from inferior things that we might give ourselves completely to this one thing: the desire of God. It is worthy of every part of our heart, mind, physical strength, and undefiled faith.

The outpourings of the Holy Spirit make us more complete in every way. We were designed to live in that glory. The equipping we experience from the gifts of Christ launches us into triumphant purpose in those outpourings, as we learn to illustrate the resurrected Christ in all we say and do. This process builds us up into strength, purity, authority, faith, and great unity. The impact of our life in Christ changes how people around us think, and what they value. In these seasons, culture itself becomes transformed because the values and appetites of the citizens change. The change happens from within. And in that climate, the climate created by His manifest presence upon His liberated people, beauty and wonder are restored.

> *But we all, with unveiled face, beholding as in a mirror the glory of the Lord, are being **transformed** into the same image from glory to glory, just as **by the Spirit** of the Lord* (2 Corinthians 3:18 NKJV).

To hunger for anything less than living in His glory is to sell ourselves short in the divine design. Jesus is returning for a glorious Church; a Church of the presence, illustrating the reality of Heaven here and now. This is our hour to stand in the glory of God, and see what might be possible in our lifetime . . . us becoming *a mature man.*

To hunger for anything less than living in His glory is to sell ourselves short.

NOTES

1. Foreword by Lou Engle for Larry Sparks, comp., *Ask for the Rain* (Shippensburg, PA: Destiny Image Publishers, 2016), 9.

ABOUT BILL JOHNSON

BILL JOHNSON is a fifth-generation pastor with a rich heritage in the Holy Spirit. Bill and his wife, Beni, are the senior leaders of Bethel Church in Redding, California, and serve a growing number of churches that cross denominational lines, demonstrate power, and partner for revival. Bill's vision is for all believers to experience God's presence and operate in the miraculous—as expressed in his bestselling books *When Heaven Invades Earth* and *Hosting the Presence*. The Johnsons have three children and eleven grandchildren.

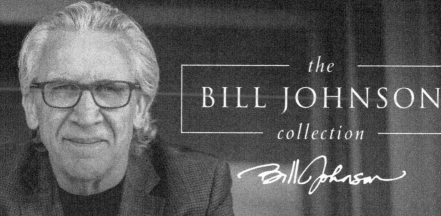

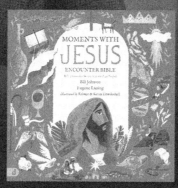

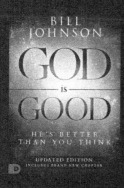

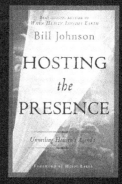

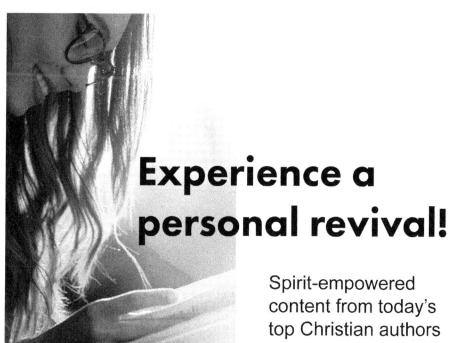

Printed by Printforce, United Kingdom